Best Beginnings

for Your Baby and You

CONCEPTION, PREGNANCY, BIRTH AND LOOKING AHEAD

Sarah Woodhouse

HELPING PARENTS SHINE

RIGHT FROM THE START

The information and advice presented in this e-book has been reviewed and approved by
medical doctors and childcare professionals. It should not, however, substitute for the advice of
your own doctor or trained healthcare professional. You are advised to consult with them with
regard to all matters that may require medical attention or diagnosis. The publisher and author
specifically disclaim any responsibility for any risk which may be claimed or incurred
as a consequence of the practice of anything presented in this book.

See www.right-from-the-start.org for details of further
Right from the Start books, products and parent support.

Matador
9 Priory Business Park,
Wistow Road, Kibworth Beauchamp,
Leicestershire, LE8 0RX
Tel: 0116 279 2299
Email: books@troubador.co.uk
Web: www.troubador.co.uk/matador
Twitter: @matadorbooks

ISBN 978 1789018 806

British Library Cataloguing in Publication Data.
A catalogue record for this book is available from the British Library.

Printed and bound by CPI Group (UK) Ltd, Croydon, CR0 4YY
Typeset in 11pt Georgia by Troubador Publishing Ltd, Leicester, UK

Matador is an imprint of Troubador Publishing Ltd

This book is dedicated to Emma Barlow,
whose loving energy, joy and vision inspired me to start writing.

Her faith and courage shone out for all who knew her.

She died on 22 January 2003 aged thirty-two.

Right from the Start's logo of the Dolphin and Child comes from the 18 foot bronze statue by David Wynne on London's Chelsea Embankment, by the River Thames.

The child and dolphin playing together symbolises the trust, love, adventure and sense of unity in all creation which each of us should be able to understand and enjoy — and share with each other — from earliest childhood to the end of our lives.

Contents

Acknowledgements

Many people have been involved in the planning and drafting of this book, some people perhaps without knowing it.

For their extraordinary knowledge, wisdom and humanity and the support and encouragement they have given me, my deepest gratitude must go to Dr Joseph Chilton Pearce, Dr Frank Lake, Nim Barnes at Foresight and Anna Verwaal. Special thanks to Anna – midwife, birth educator and birth photographer – for her sensitive and intimate sepia photographs.

The brilliant minds and loving energy of these people have motivated and taught me so much over many years as the Helping Parents Shine – Right from the Start project developed, and this book was being drafted.

Warmest gratitude to Maggie Howell whose birth preparation support and natal hypnotherapy gives such comfort to mothers. And to Dr Rosie Knowles who set up and runs the Sheffield Sling Surgery. Her advice and help in drafting the chapter on babywearing and providing the photographs for this chapter have been outstanding.

I am warmly indebted to Sheila Kitzinger, Andrew Chevalier, Phillipa Howell (Homeopath), Melanie Cook, Harvey Karp and Margo Sunderland for their stimulation and help. I would like to thank Sheila Kitzinger in particular for her original permission to draw anything from her book, *Being Born*, including some of the photographs of a baby's development in the womb by Lennart Nilsson.

I thank the Brain Gym® Foundation UK for permission to describe some simplified Brain Gym® exercises in Chapter 3. Warm thanks to Claire Dolby for her sensitive and personal story, 'The Birth and Death of My Baby' in Appendix 7.

I have also drawn gratefully from the research findings of Jaak Panksepp, Alan Stone, Joseph E. LeDoux and Christopher Walsh at the Boston Children's Hospital.

Perhaps most importantly, my heartfelt thanks must go to all the parents, grandparents, midwives, health visitors, family friends, neighbours and generous strangers who shared their experiences, their feelings and their hopes with me. Their stories and descriptions are what truly bring this book to life and make it a shared endeavour.

Special thanks also to Deirdre Youngs and Patrick Tomlinson for their editing expertise. Deirdre has been a matchless adviser and co-author as well as editor. Her continuous, loyal support and involvement throughout have been a source of creative inspiration and joy to me. Final and warm gratitude also to Noël Riley and Caroline Bushell for their devoted efforts to perfect and polish the manuscript and bring it all together so well.

Sarah Woodhouse

Introduction

If we hope to create
a non-violent world
where respect and kindness
replace fear and hatred
We must begin
with how we treat each other
at the beginning of life.
For that is where
our deepest patterns are set.
From these roots
grow fear and alienation
– or love and trust.

Suzanne Arms

I DIDN'T KNOW ANY BABIES WHEN I WAS GROWING UP!

More people than ever before go through their own childhood without ever holding a baby in their arms or helping a toddler walk and talk. This can be a disadvantage when you find yourself expecting your first child.

This *Best Beginnings* book is for reading before your child is born, ideally before or as soon as you conceive. Keep it nearby so you can re-read any part of it which you feel might help you. Share those pages with your midwife and someone close to you.

> *I can't imagine what it would be like having a baby to think about all the time, every single day. I mean, I wouldn't know where to start. It could drive you mad!*
> **Karen**

Best Beginnings for Your Baby and You is a friendly, comforting, 'stand-in' when you need it and there is no one close by to help you.

This book is full of pictures, shared stories and experiences to remind us that we are all in this together, doing our best to be good parents, needing to learn from each other and help each other. This puts into perspective, and helps us cope with, those difficulties which life may throw at us.

This book is not just for expectant and new parents, grandparents and helpful and friendly neighbours. It is also for midwives and health visitors in training or at work and everyone else involved in any way with mothers and their babies from the very beginning.

It is written to be a 'bridge', allowing a greater flow of understanding and trust between all these people so that confidence, happiness and gentle, nurturing skills can build in young families, right from the start, even when life's circumstances are difficult. This will deeply affect the way a child's personality, spirit and love of others will blossom during childhood – and the rest of his life.

Your patience, steadiness and loving calm are the greatest gifts you can give to your baby – far more precious than gold! This happens through the ways you hold him, touch him, kiss him, talk to him, care for him from the day he is born – and introduce him to the community in which you live.

Parents hold up the sky for their children

WHY IS SUPPORT FOR PARENTS – ESPECIALLY MOTHERS – SO IMPORTANT?

Every mother needs enough financial support so that she is not driven by money worries or loneliness to go back to work within the first years, leaving her baby or toddler in a nursery, often with different helpers coming and going and no one-to-one carer to give him full and tender attention during the hours of seperation.

When both Mum and Dad are working for half or the whole day, how can they have enough practice to understand their baby, become close and loving parents and be caught up in the excitement of his amazing development?

> *The decision to have a child is momentous. It is to decide forever to have your heart go walking around outside your body.*
> **Elizabeth Stone**

Right from the Start has drawn from impeccable research and the vision of many world-renowned professionals alongside the experiences, skills, stories and understanding of a great number of parents, grandparents, midwives and health visitors. All this will help you to recognise the extraordinary intelligence, sensitivity and understanding that are there in your baby even before birth, and your baby's playfulness and efforts to communicate with you from the moment of birth.

WHAT ARE THE LONG-TERM EFFECTS OF SENSITIVE AND CONFIDENT PARENTING?

> *If every parent, new and old, had a chance to read through Best Beginnings for Your Baby and You to talk about the things in this book which caught their imagination, and share whatever made good sense to them with their midwife or health visitor, we'd at least make a start to bring about the changes needed so desperately – more kindness and peace in the world.*
> **Deirdre, a birth specialist**

Family research shows that, through lack of support, an alarming number of parents slip into serious marriage or partnership problems or family breakdown within five years of the birth of their first child.

www.nct.org.uk/parenting/changes-your-relationships-after-having-baby

Dr Joseph Chilton Pearce, MA, neurologist and author, who died in 2016, passionately believed that 'we have the chance to erase all forms of violence through a proper approach to pregnancy, birth and the first years of life'.

> *I'm proud of many things in my life but nothing beats being a mother. It helps me to be kind again and again and again!*
> **Fanny**

Note: In order to avoid the awkwardness of using 'he or she' throughout this book, we have chosen to use 'he' throughout. This also avoids any confusion when referring to a mum and her baby daughter in the same paragragh!

Two more books in the Right from the Start series for new parents will follow soon:
Best Beginnings: The Amazing Development of Your Baby in the First Nine Months
Best Beginnings: The First Three Years – a Very Special Time

~ CHAPTER 1 ~

The Peace of the World Begins With Babies

There's no need to think about cultural differences or what education or money we've got or not got. Mums are mums the world over. Dads are dads and babies are babies. The things that matter most to us and the things we most need are the same, all the world over.
Pauli, a midwife

I've done it!

What happens to us at conception, during our months in the womb and at our birth has a profound effect on the rest of our life.

Anna Verwaal's TED Talk explains this beautifully for us:
www.youtube.com/watch?v=bZ6gLGCy84o

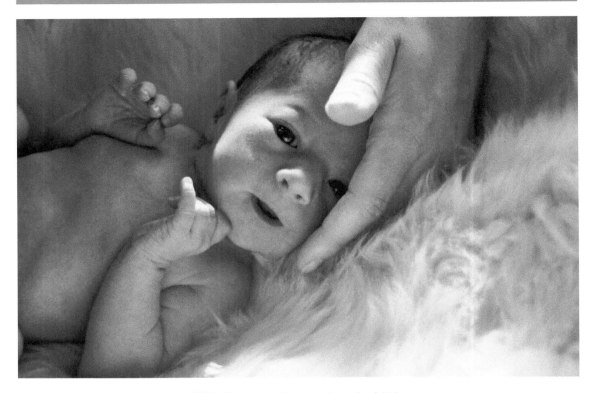

With Dad, two hours after the birth

BABIES ARE THE SEEDS OF LIFE, BELONGING TO US ALL

♥ All children from their first beginnings have special vulnerability, understanding and sensitivity.

♥ All children have special wisdom. They have instinctive, inside knowledge of how things should be.

♥ Children have their own special strengths, special energy, and a special urge to grow in every way and to share their lives with others. They expect to love and be loved, and long to be capable and creative.

♥ They have a powerful need to feel at the centre of their family. They need to be 'the apple of someone's eye' and to be welcomed and cared about by their community.

♥ They need to feel that they belong. They need to feel valued.

♥ They need to grow up with a sense of connection to the whole of creation. Children's happiness often comes from feeling an instinctive unity with every living thing that catches their attention and fascinates them. This sense of 'oneness' can be a powerful feeling in young children.

All these needs stay with each one of us throughout our lives.

My first memory of delight and amazement was when I was three years old. I was standing outside holding onto an old wooden table which was wet because it had been raining. My eyes were just level with the edge of the table and I was watching a snail coming straight towards me. When it was right in front of me, it suddenly stretched up its tiny black eyes on their long waving stalks and looked all over my face. I had never seen a snail before. He had never seen me before! But I knew straightaway that he saw I was me! He was saying, 'I can see you! Hello!'
Dale Mather

A DVD called *The Healing of Birth* by Elmer Postle can give you further insights and encouragement:

http://wholebeingfilms.com/product/healing-birth/

PARENTS, ESPECIALLY MUMS, HOLD UP THE SKY FOR THEIR CHILDREN

Such good things will happen for your baby – and for you – when a loving bond grows ever stronger between you. These early feelings of safety and of happiness we have with our parents while we are babies, toddlers and young children will greatly influence the rest of our lives.

These are some older children's memories of their parents' love for them:

My mother is medium-sized, brown in colour and as cool as a cucumber. Her hair is red and thick. She has a proud walk, and is as tender as a chicken. A rose is as beautiful as my mother, and she is as fresh as a daisy, and as strong as an ox.

When I grow up I would like to be as beautiful as my mother. And have the beautiful ways she has. My mother is more precious than gold.
Carmen (11)

I love my mother. She gave birth to me and to her I owe my life.
Papageorgiou (9)

She laughs when I laugh, she cries when I cry, she gets excited when I get excited.
I can't say more about her except that she lives for me and I live for her.
Josephides (10)

Dad carries me on his shoulders to the allotment. We dig together and get dirty.
Stephen (4)

The things my mum does for me are uncountable. She has been helping me hours on end ever since I was born.
Mark (8)

If it was not for Mum we would look like a sack of potatoes.
Tony (7)

I like doing things with my dad. He pulls faces to make me laugh.
Charlie (6)

Whatever my mum does, I still love her.
Barry (10)

OUR WORLD OF RAPID CHANGES AND UNCERTAINTIES

These days parenting, especially parenting without loving grandparents and friendly neighbours, is in some ways harder than it was 200 years ago. More and more parents are struggling on their own, perhaps anxious, exhausted or even feeling angry. If there is not enough practical and emotional support to comfort and encourage them, their anxiety and frustration easily builds up and is handed on as impatience and unkindness, through no fault of their own, to their babies and children. Their children suffer in turn and can grow insecure, out of control, or even shut down. They may be struggling with loneliness, uncertainty and fear. These three emotions can quickly turn into anger.

> *Being and feeling cared about and loved lies at the root of feeling happy. Happy people can do so much to be friends to others and build happiness around them. Mothers, especially if they are alone and feeling unsupported and anxious, need to watch out for and find happy people in their community to talk to and be with.*
> **A community nurse**

> *Parents need greater emotional support and help than ever before. This support needs to come from all sides: from family members; from neighbours; from professionals; and from the wider community. It must also come from a government which recognises the importance of parenting and passes laws which answer the true needs of parents.*
> **A Member of Parliament, UK**

A STRONG COMMUNITY AROUND YOU

Where the extended family is out of reach, and when there is no husband or partner to help you care for your baby, the challenge will be how to become involved with the community you live in – in ways which will help you get to know other people well and find lasting friends.

Explore all the possibilities in your area. Ask at your medical centre or clinic and the public library. Try the internet (for example, www.netmums.com) and local newspapers, and discover if there is, within reach of you:

Introducing a piglet to the goats in a city farm

- Baby and toddler groups
- Activity groups, such as music and dance
- A local children's centre
- Birthlight or other yoga centres for children
- Allotments
- City farms
- NCT (www.nct.org.uk/parenting)

Growing happiness will come if you can discover real friends among the older generation as well as those of your own age. To give and receive affection, to get close enough to find shared interests and trust with people of all ages – who were perhaps strangers to you not long ago – will make life richer and more fun. There will be helping hands when you need them and a chance to learn from each other's skills, share your own discoveries and develop your own best instincts.

It was as if a neighbour who I called 'Auntie Bessie' almost saved my life. I wasn't well after the birth and I was a long way from my parents. When I was unsure about what to do with my new baby, her practical nature and her smiling face were always there for me. She made me and my baby feel secure.
Muriel

CONCEIVING YOUR BABY

It can make a great difference to every baby if both parents are in good health and spirits before they conceive.

Sexual excitement!

There's more to sex than sex – even at those times when sex may be a big priority in our lives and ruling our thoughts and behaviour to a great degree. There is a deep-down 'knowing' in our bodies, even when our minds are distracted, that sex is finally to create new life.

There is also, in most women, a deep-down 'longing', even when contraception is being used long term, or drink or drugs are interfering with the instincts of our own bodies that, one day, we might want a baby.

There is also the wonder of birth for most of us. It is the surging of hormones which transforms each of us from *being* a woman into *becoming* a mother. This is the experience of a lifetime for both parents and is perhaps the biggest and best growing and learning change that will ever happen to us.

> *Loving is the first thing children learn – I wish life would teach them never to forget it.*
> **Nanette Newman**

The health of *both* parents, starting in the months before trying for a baby, has a direct effect on the conception, growth in the womb and full-term birth of a baby, as well as the baby's ongoing health. It can also make all the difference to your recovery from the birth and how you settle down together.

Before you conceive your baby

In 1979 a charity called Foresight pioneered an exploration into our fundamental health through years of dedicated research into the effects on our bodies of nutrition, alcohol, smoking, drugs, levels of toxic metals, pesticides, food additives and other environmental hazards.

Nim Barnes founded and directed Foresight for almost forty years.

She developed a programme (which sadly had to close in 2017) to help both parents ensure that they are in good health, ideally even before they conceive their child. It provides sensible, achievable information and advice on how to do this. Foresight proved that it is really important to conceive our babies on purpose instead of by chance. This way we give them and ourselves the best possible pregnancy and future together. Even making small adjustments to what we eat and drink and stopping the use of certain substances can dramatically change our ability to conceive.

Foresight helped parents to overcome infertility, miscarriage, premature birth, stillbirth, low birth weight, birth defects and many other problems, such as postnatal depression, breastfeeding difficulties and poor resistance to infection.

Difficulty conceiving and completing *your* pregnancy?

Both would-be parents need to be checked out for genital, urinary and other infections. Some infections may be present without any symptoms. Every one of them can be successfully treated.

A hair analysis for both parents is able to show whether or not there is an excess of heavy (toxic) metals in their bodies and/or a shortage of any essential nutrients.

A healing and cleansing programme can be put in place to treat any infection and to remove any toxic metals present in the bloodstream. Necessary food supplements can be introduced to correct any imbalance of minerals and to ensure that there is no shortage of essential vitamins.

Later, both parents can be retested, and the cleansing and additional supplement programme re-adjusted and repeated until tests show that the level of the overall

HOW TO CONCEIVE
Healthy Babies
The Natural Way

Nim Barnes

health of both parents is so improved that their chances of conceiving, enjoying a complications-free pregnancy and giving birth full term to a healthy and contented baby will be high.

One way and another, this 'foresight' can make a big difference to your commitment to each other, the strength of your loving relationship and, most of all, to the health and life of the baby that you are hoping for.

> *I had a daughter born safely after a normal pregnancy but I developed postnatal depression when she was about four months old. We were living in the Netherlands and I was still ill a year later, despite progesterone and homeopathic treatment for months. I then had two miscarriages.*
>
> *I will never forget the encouragement and hope that came in the letter from Nim Barnes with the results of my hair analysis. I had severe zinc deficiency (among other things) which I was told could explain both the miscarriages and my depression. 'Everything can be put right' was her message, and so it proved.*
>
> *The vitamin and mineral regime was begun, including whole, fresh, organic foods as much as possible. I was retested twenty weeks later. Then I was given the go-ahead. I conceived the very next month. My great fear was that the postnatal depression would come back – but it never did. My son is three now and thriving. We all are!*
>
> **From a letter sent to the editor of the Foresight magazine**

SERIOUS CHOICES TO THINK ABOUT...

Let's look at the not-so-good news first, to get it out of the way! Then we can look at all the good things throughout the rest of the book.

The risks for dads and their babies in a nutshell

Men who are not in good health through being on a poor diet, or smoking or drinking in excess may have far fewer sperm. Those they have will not be very good at swimming.

Dads who are smoking when their wives or partners conceive can cause some form of mental or physical disability in their baby, because quite a high proportion of their sperm will be damaged as they form, through the chemical effects of smoking.

www.fatherhoodinstitute.org/2007/fatherhood-institute-research-summary-fathers-and-smoking/

It is now known medically that such disability in a child is not necessarily the result of inherited genes or of birth trauma. Research over the last two decades paints a clearer picture of other dangers. For example, dads should avoid carrying mobile phones in their trouser pockets as there is a real possibility that this can harm their developing sperm as does drinking alcohol, smoking and taking recreational drugs.

www.ewg.org/cell-phone-radiation-damages-sperm-studies-find

The risks for mums and their babies in a nutshell

From the moment a baby is conceived, he will be at risk if his mother is smoking, drinking or taking drugs, or if his father is smoking nearby. This 'secondary' cigarette smoke also makes morning sickness more of a likelihood, which, if troublesome and lasting, can lead to a loss of the nutrients that you and your baby need.

Once a baby starts to grow in the womb, the chemicals from his mother's cigarettes and his father's smoky breath will be absorbed by him through the placenta. This can interfere with and harm the development of his brain. Harm to a baby's brain can last a lifetime. He may be less likely to be born full term, healthy, happy and easy to care for and to love.

A baby in the womb will become dependent on any recreational drug being taken by his mother – a miserable start. Drugs, just like smoking, will also interfere with the pace and completion of his growth – especially the growth of his brain. He will also suffer painful and distressing withdrawal symptoms as the supply will be cut off the moment he is born.

Caffeine

The caffeine in drinks such as coffee, Coke and non-herbal teas has been linked to miscarriage, so you may decide to avoid or drink less of these during your pregnancy and turn to water and fruit juice instead.

Alcohol in your bloodstream

Just like the 'Don't drink and drive' message, the same applies to drinking when you are growing a baby.

If you are hoping to become pregnant, or already are pregnant, get all the help and support you can and stop drinking. It can be the biggest danger of all in the early stages of pregnancy as your baby attaches to the wall of your womb and the placenta begins to develop.

There is no way of telling whether only a very small amount of alcohol or a large amount drunk in pregnancy by a mother will affect her baby. This is because each mother and each unborn baby is so different in their response to alcohol. It is therefore not possible to set a safe level of intake.

Every mother needs to know that the baby in her womb will show some signs of heart stress within a few moments of her starting to drink. It appears that babies whose mothers continue to drink through their pregnancy are more likely be born jittery and tremulous, with a weaker suck and difficulty settling into a peaceful sleep pattern. It is best to cut out alcohol entirely and so make sure your baby is truly protected.

A mother who continues to drink during her pregnancy may also find that her baby has ongoing difficulty regulating his temperature.

Alcohol can also lead to a mother's malnutrition which, of course, is passed straight on to her baby. For example, folic acid, zinc and other essential vitamins and minerals are leached out of a mother's body when she drinks alcohol, just when extra supplies are needed for her growing baby.

> *Even one drink a week during pregnancy can trigger behavioural difficulties, with a threefold rise in the risk of delinquency in older children. Even small amounts could cause permanent damage to the brain of a developing baby. Unborn babies are affected because their liver is not sufficiently developed to process alcohol in their mother's blood, which can stay in their tiny bodies up to six times longer.*
> **Dr Mukherjee, St George's Hospital Medical School, London**

The greatest harm

When the effect on a baby of his mother's drinking is severe it is known as Foetal Alcohol Syndrome. This means there will probably be damage to the baby's heart, liver, pancreas and joints, as well as to his brain. This will result in poor growth, hyperactivity and possibly obesity and allergies later in life.

Heavy metal!

Heavy metals, such as mercury, cadmium and lead in our bodies, except in the minutest amounts, are poisonous, especially for our babies. Lead is one of the heaviest and most poisonous.

Lead

Lead has been around in the earth's crust forever but it has only started to contaminate us since it has been mined increasingly over the last few hundred years and used in petrol, in manufacturing, particularly in paint and pottery and battery-making processes. It is also with us in roofing and old plumbing pipes. It gets itself into our water, our food and even into the air we breathe – through petrol exhaust fumes. Unborn babies and young children absorb this lead more readily than adults and the polluting effect on their brains can be serious.

Mercury

The main sources of mercury poisoning are through amalgam fillings in dental cavities, also from eating tuna and swordfish. Mercury is used as a preservative for wheat seed planting and the run-off from these fields can pollute water supplies.

Ask for porcelain fillings in your teeth and avoid tuna or swordfish because these huge, long-living fish accumulate mercury in their bodies over time.

Cadmium

Cadmium is present in tiny amounts in all soil and rocks. It is used in metal coatings, batteries, some pigments and as a stabiliser for plastics. It causes cancer when absorbed. Most damaging of all for an unborn or newborn baby is the high levels of cadmium in cigarette smoke from smoking parents. They will have twice the amount of toxic metals in their bodies and therefore on their skin as non-smokers.

What can be done?

Milk and egg white bind with and remove some heavy metals such as lead and mercury from our bodies. They help to prevent them harming us and our unborn babies.

Eating garlic, onions, ginger, curry leaf, soya beans, grapes, tomatoes and taking zinc supplements and drinking green tea all help to remove cadmium from our bodies.

Pesticides and chemical fertilisers

Foods grown with chemical fertilisers are missing some valuable nutrients. Many factory-made foods which have been over-processed for a longer shelf-life prevent us from being truly well. They may contain fruit and vegetables grown with chemical fertilisers. They may also have absorbed the residue from pesticides. We often can't choose exactly what we are eating in a packaged 'ready meal'. Eating organic foods does a great deal to reduce the levels of unhealthy chemicals in our blood.

Growth hormones and antibiotics

Crowded intensive farming methods mean that a great deal of the cheaper meat in the shops may be from animals who have gained weight fast through being fed growth hormones and who have been protected from disease by being fed antibiotics. Remnants of these distorting hormones and these antibiotics can still be there when we eat the meat, even after cooking. The latest research suggests that many of our physical problems, such as obesity, may stem from eating meat from animals and eggs from chickens which have been fed on artificial and unnatural foodstuffs.

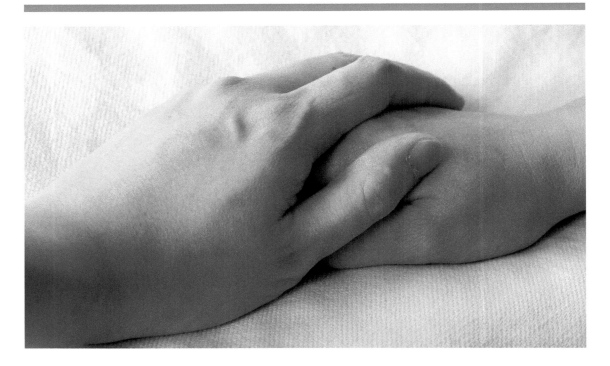

UNEXPLAINED INFERTILITY

'Infertile', such a cruel word for the lifelessness of my world, for my longing each day to have good news. I look at the hundreds of lambs and other parents. Why can't that be me?
Ellie

A programme based in America called Life FertilityCare, maximises the chances of conceiving by getting the body's reproductive tissues into the most balanced state of health possible. This, ideally, should be considered and followed up as a first choice before IVF. The programme is offered over twelve months. Whereas Foresight focused on pre-conceptual care, the Life FertilityCare programme, based on Natural Procreative Technology (NaPro), goes further, offering specific treatments including hormone injections. NaPro can solve infertility, recurrent miscarriage and teach natural family planning: www.lifefertilitycare.co.uk

~ **CHAPTER 2** ~

I'm pregnant! What am I feeling?

Birth is not only about making babies. Birth is about making mothers – strong, competent, capable mothers who trust themselves and know their inner strength.
Barbara Katz Rothman

FEELINGS AND INTUITION

Some of us know when we are pregnant by intuition – even before we have a pregnancy test. Intuition is like an inner voice of certainty. It comes more from our heart than from our head. When our heart is open to loving and caring, we listen more to our intuition. Love and intuition go hand-in-hand.

Expectant mums and dads often become more intuitively sensitive to each other, as well as to people around them.

This extra sensitivity grows in us to help us feel closer to each other and cope with big changes when and as they happen. But intuition can only come to us – and work for us – when we are able to slow down and relax.

Your emotions – your strong feelings – and your intuition are doubly important when you have a baby growing inside you. They will affect how your baby will grow, especially how well his brain will grow, and therefore the way he will respond to life after he is born. Your peaceful feelings and happiness, or any continuously troubling thoughts you have, will reach your child, however tiny he still is.

Babies feel part of, and relate to, their mother as soon as they start to grow in the womb. Before very long, they will be picking up the warmth or lack of warmth in the relationship between their mum and their dad.

Babies are in communication with their mother and father from the womb. Little signals are travelling backwards and forwards continually between all three of you.

WHAT'S GOING ON IN YOUR HEAD AND YOUR HEART?

What are you thinking?

This is the best thing that's ever happened to me!
Can this be real?
I'm so excited!
My mum and dad'll be over the moon!
'What shall I do? Who can I tell?'
This is such a big mistake!
I feel so shocked and scared.

Does a wave of anxiety sweep over you every time you wake up and remember you're pregnant or does a surge of joy and hope? Anxiety and excitement are often closely linked together – a sense of the big changes and the unknown lying ahead.

You may have some or all of these feelings at different times in the first few days or weeks. So much will depend on your present circumstances – the reaction of your baby's father, the reaction of the family around you and your friends, and being able to talk through your feelings with someone you trust and who loves you. It will also depend on your practical, day-to-day needs.

Sometimes you may feel full of hope and overjoyed to imagine a baby in your arms before the year is out. The very next day you may wake up feeling worried about such a big responsibility and wondering how your life is going to change. You may be thinking:

What will the birth be like? How much will it hurt?

Will my baby be born OK?

Having a newborn baby to attend to, day and night – what will that be like?

How will I cope? Who will be there to help me?

Will it be hard to manage with not much money to spare?

Will I love my baby? Will my baby love me?

Will my family be there for me?

Will my friends forget about me?

HOW CAN WE BEGIN TO LOVE OUR NEWLY CONCEIVED CHILD IF OUR THOUGHTS AND FEELINGS ABOUT BEING PREGNANT ARE STILL MIXED UP?

The miniscule child you are carrying needs you, as soon as possible, to think of him as a real person already. Growing your love for your growing baby in the womb will make such a difference to your pregnancy and his life ahead. It will also help you feel more confident for the birth – you will be sharing the journey together. When your child is born, you'll already 'know' each other.

Taking the first step might be to imagine your own birth journey, however many years ago that was...

Finding time to think... in a quiet and peaceful place

During the first few days after you have had your pregnancy confirmed, try to find half an hour or so when you can be alone and still – to think about *yourself*. Perhaps you can sit in your favourite chair, or outside under a tree, or warm in bed? If you are inside, shut the door, draw the curtains and have just a reading light switched on. Unplug the phone or switch off your mobile. It might help if you listen to some quiet and peaceful music.

How was it when you were conceived? Could you shut your eyes and let your imagination take you back to your earliest beginnings and see it all happening? The way we each develop is amazing and wonderful, yet many of us have never stopped to think through and understand the way of our own birth.

Thinking through your own beginnings and seeing in your mind's eye how your own life began can help to steady your thoughts and feelings. Taking time to do this can help you to feel calmer and more hopeful about your pregnancy now and your baby's birth in a few months.

If the circumstances of your own conception and birth, or your present circumstances, are distressing, you might need someone close and understanding to share this birth journey with you.

> *When I was conceived, I was unwanted and then given away when I was born. This brings up a lot of pain for me but now I'm having my own baby, it's different and it feels like it's healing something in me.*
> **Julie**

Here is a helpful and gentle way to start putting things into perspective.

IMAGINING YOUR OWN BIRTH JOURNEY

As soon as you're warm and comfortable, breathing steadily and peacefully, your imagination can take over.

You could read your own birth story – as described here – slowly and silently to yourself, or out loud with long enough pauses for your own ears to listen to your own voice speaking. The pauses will also give you time to imagine it happening, step by step. Otherwise, you might be able to record a slow reading of it in your own voice so that you can listen to it in your own words with your eyes shut.

Where am I? Just imagine!

I'm here – a tiny egg smaller than a pinhead – launching from the soft ovary nest where I have lain all my mother's life. The egg which is me had already grown inside my mother as she grew in her mother's womb. All that time ago, the egg that became me was there, carried everywhere, even in my grandmother when she was pregnant with my mother... and then everywhere, all her life, by my mother. Amazing!

What does it feel like to launch off from the ovary... the one special egg chosen from around 400? Not one is the same. I am a single cell popped out of my mother's ovary like a seed from a pod. I hold inside me inherited memories, like faint echoes, of both my mother's life, and my grandmother's life – I carry with me some of the indelible experiences and sensations of their lifetimes.

All these years and years of stillness and now, all of a sudden, I'm released. I'm off on my journey to conception.

The journey

Tiny hairs, like eyelashes, pull and roll me into the mouth of the fallopian tube so I don't get lost in the great cavity around me. I slip into the wide space of this pathway, down, down towards my mother's womb. I'm on the move, edged along, little by little, by the continuous movements of these tiny hairs. I'm like a grain of sand tumbled slowly along a river bed amongst the swaying weeds. Soft and silent and dark. Stopping and starting. Slipping and sticking. I still have far, far to go. Nutrients, from the food my mother ate before I was conceived, are packed around me to feed me on my journey. Everything feels right. Everything feels new, warm and welcoming... and, for the first time in my life I am on the move.

What messages am I carrying with me?

I am carrying a genetic code, a kind of blueprint, passed down to me from generation to generation of my mother's family.

I am also carrying a lifetime of her experiences, habits, behaviour and feelings. All the electrical and chemical messages from her body and from her mind are in me too.

I was there inside her and part of her all the time.

What's going to happen next?

My mother's history and influence is carried in me for my spirit to do what I like with.

My father's history is coming to meet me, also for my spirit to do what I like with.

Where am I now? I am still here, rolling down the fallopian tube towards the womb. But, something else is beginning to happen. The movement of the trembling hairs around me and the flow of the river start to reverse. The movement and flow are now upwards, carrying some of my father's sperm towards me. Infinitely smaller than me, they are made each day by the million. Each one takes sixty-four days to be fully grown. It takes 2,000 movements of the tail of a sperm to swim a centimetre.

Just imagine! About 40 million sperm may have been released into my mother's body but only one will be the winner. There's a big race on to get to me first.

Hundreds of my father's sperm come to surround me. Which single sperm will win and fuse with me? At last, just one of them manages to burrow deeply through my outer skin, to my very centre.

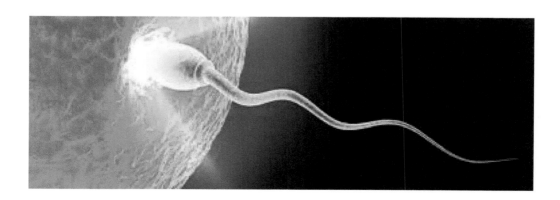

In less than a second, I burst into life!

Instantly, I am filled with energy and activity, sparked off by all the new information from the sperm fused with me! My own life is beginning.

First, the cell that I am slowly draws itself in across its middle – like a minute hourglass – until all at once it becomes two. Then each divides again and again, faster and faster. Each new pair of cells is more of me.

For the next three or four days I multiply and multiply, like excitement bubbling. Now I have become a tiny bundle of shining cells. I look like a silvery blackberry. And, all the while, the tiny hairs are, once more, rolling and guiding me as I grow, towards my new home.

Finding my home

Suddenly I reach the end of the flowing stream and tip over the edge into a huge, velvet cavern. I'm floating free in space like an astronaut. I'm floating and growing, growing and floating. But I need to land now and feel still and safe. I can't grow anymore on my own. I am big enough and strong enough now to bury myself in the soft wall of my mother's womb.

So, on the seventh day, stillness comes to me again. I choose my spot, near to the top, close to one of my mother's main arteries. Her body knows I am there and will anchor me and feed me.

I turn all my energy to becoming a child. Now I'm the size of a thumbnail. I grow and grow and grow. Very soon I have a heart which is beating steadily, a brain which grows faster than any other part of me and the beginning of arms and legs, then fingers and toes.

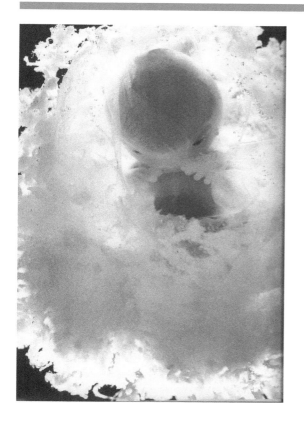

Later, I begin to hear the soothing sounds of my mother's body – her heart beating, her breathing, the flow of her blood and the gurgling of her digestion. Now I can hear her voice, clear but muffled, and sometimes other voices more faintly. I listen and listen. These sounds are so familiar – they make me feel safe and alive.

I open my mouth, sip the water around me and can taste the flavour of the different things my mother has eaten.

I begin to touch and feel my mouth, my legs, my head, with my fingers. I roll over and feel the firmness of the umbilical cord. I move each finger and toe. I invent my own games. I dance my own dance.

I play with the soft billowing curtain of the sac holding the water around me. I curl and straighten myself, push, kick and shove to make it stretch and flex. I sip the water touching my mouth and suck my thumb.

Then my eyes peep open and just occasionally, I can dimly, dimly begin to see a faint pink glow and the movement of my hands.

I'm so big now; I can't kick anymore or stretch my arms. I'm curled up tight. Every day it's harder to move. I wonder what will happen next?

When you have finished this journey in your imagination, sit quietly for another moment or two, get up slowly, feel your feet on the ground and perhaps have a drink of water or a cup of tea.

What does being pregnant feel like to you now? In what ways would you like to change the way you are feeling?

> *My friend came and read the birth journey story to me while I lay on the sofa and listened to her. At first we got the giggles a bit but she kept on slowly to the end. It was OK. It was good. I can't quite describe what happened. I think it helped me catch up with myself and I felt happier somehow.*
>
> **Sara, with her pregnancy just confirmed**

Expectant and new dads

How do you want to be as a father? In the same way, looking back and searching out memories of their own birth and childhood – by asking and talking – can help future fathers to think ahead with imagination and hopefulness. Fathers-To-Be (www. fatherstobe.org) gives wonderful and knowledgeable support to expectant and new dads. This will help you to feel closer to the mother of your child, closer to your unborn or newborn baby – and also understand the roles of, and feel supported by, all those professionals caring for your family.

Who was Dr Frank Lake?

Dr Frank Lake was an exceptionally gentle and loving doctor and psychiatrist. He developed an extraordinary skill in helping women at conception and during pregnancy and childbirth, so that their experiences could be more joyful and complete and less fearful or uncertain. The exercise of imagining your own birth journey comes from Frank. He used it with the mothers he was caring for like a kind of meditation. Frank understood how important a mother's loving feelings were for her unborn child, from the earliest days and throughout her pregnancy. Some mothers may need help before these loving feelings can begin to grow. This could be because what happened to them when they were in the womb, during their birth and the first few months of life was not as full of understanding, care and love as they needed.

Although Frank has now died, his insights, his healing skills and his loving kindness live on in others. His work is carried on through the Bridge Pastoral Foundation www. bridgepastoral.org.uk and also through the vision of other pioneers, such as Dr William Emerson and Dr Raymond Castellino.

Birth-like experiences will repeat in our lives

Frank describes how the whole step-by-step journey towards a new life, from the moment of release from the ovary, may be repeated over and over again in different ways and at different times in our lives – like going to school, leaving home, changing jobs, finding a partner, getting married and moving house.

When we give ourselves time to think slowly and carefully about this, our very first journey, we shall be able later to notice the same pattern repeating itself in our lives. This can help us absorb such changes more readily and peacefully.

First day at school

FIRST MEMORIES

The ability of each one of us to recall earliest memories – even of sensations we experienced in the womb and during our birth – is still with us. These memories and sensations were carried, not just in our rapidly growing brains but in every cell and nerve in every part of our body, and especially in the nerves and cells of our skin. Some people find this hard to believe, simply because such memories faded away before we were old enough to have words to describe them. They may then have been buried so deep that they will probably never again rise to the surface of our minds. However, our earliest memories, although hidden away, may still show up later in our feelings and our behaviour.

Frank Lake understood this and worked to help many mothers to recover from the hurtful effects of any bad and sad memories of their own time in the womb, their own birth and their own early childhood. He did this by helping mothers to bring these buried memories to the surface, talking about them together and so lessening their impact. He helped mothers realise that there was nothing wrong with them, that it was only their own sensitivity and what they had undergone that had been hurting them, perhaps for years and years.

Frank Lake and many others also recognised that mothers who have a spiritual understanding and inner faith provide an atmosphere for their unborn and newborn babies which are second to none. It will support a calmer and happier pregnancy and an easier birth, and will ensure a deep mother-child bond.

Thinking about your own experiences, in the past as well as now, and talking about it with close family and friends, as well as your midwife, will make it easier for you to recognise and to ask the right people for the help you may need. This might include support towards healing a troubled past, as well as help towards a happy and hopeful pregnancy and birth.

The ideas, stories, images, interesting discoveries and useful knowledge that follow here may help you answer some of your own questions. They are there to introduce you to a new way of looking towards the future at this special time in your life. They are a sharing of the thoughts and valuable experiences of many people.

What do you think are the things needed by everyone, but especially by a woman when she gets pregnant and starts a family?

These answers came up most frequently from women about their pregnancy:

'I needed to feel safe.'

'I needed to feel connected to other people, especially to the father of my baby and to my mum.'

'I needed to feel in control of what I was thinking and doing – like being confident and knowing my own mind, whatever was happening to me.'

'I needed lots of loving attention so I would be able to cope with being pregnant - especially feeling sick.'

'I needed to be kissed and cuddled often, especially when I was feeling scared about the birth.'

'I needed to think about and imagine a good future.'

'I needed more than usual to be able to tell someone who loved me about my day. It helped me to simmer down.'

WHAT ARE YOU EATING THESE DAYS?

Your growing baby will soon be able to taste the different foods you eat from sipping the changing amniotic fluid flowing round his face every day. This will affect his health now and in the future. When you wean him he will enjoy the taste of food which you have eaten during pregnancy and be less willing to eat anything that tastes 'different'.

Could you make a big effort for his sake to change your eating habits – if this is needed – enough to ensure that throughout pregnancy you are eating the following:

1. Whole unadulterated food

Eaten as it grew in the ground or on a tree, whole unadulterated food has all the enzymes needed for its own digestion. The wholeness is also important because the vitamins, minerals and trace elements usually lie in, or very close to, the skin of most fruits and vegetables.

Fruit is a particularly valuable source of enzymes for the absorption of nutrients and is therefore best eaten before rather than after a meal, or as a snack on its own.

Eat the whole of everything whenever possible. For example, scrub and boil potatoes in their skins. Mash them in their skins too (they taste more interesting!).

Eat organic fruit and veg as much as possible so you *can* eat the skins without the risk of absorbing remnants of pesticides and agro-chemicals.

Eat green-leaf veg every day if possible, as this is proven to help your baby's growing brain and give protection from serious diseases in adult life. www.bbc.co.uk/news/magazine-34222452. Also see Appendix 1: Protecting Your Baby's Health in the Womb.

Eat unpolished brown rice, bread made from wholemeal flour, spelt flour and granary flour, and cereals made from whole grains (unadulterated!).

Beware of any factory-made food that is labelled 'no added sugar/salt' or 'added vitamins'. Chemical sweeteners are depressive and, to some people, become brain poisons. 'Added vitamins' means (a) that they are expensive foods and (b) the added vitamins are not so easily assimilated because the balance has gone.

https://bodyecology.com/articles/why_pregnant mothers_avoid_junk_food.php

2. Raw fruit and vegetables

Eat a piece of fruit before a main meal and also add chopped fruit of all kinds, raisins, nuts and seeds to salads to make them more interesting and tasty. Vegetables, whether raw or lightly cooked, are even more important to you and your baby than fruit. If cost is a problem, could you just eat smaller portions? Influenced by the bombardment of advertising, many of us eat much more than we need – and often the wrong things.

3. Fats and oils

Vegetable oils should be kept in a cool, dark place because, apart from coconut and palm oil, they oxidise and lose their 'goodness'. It is best to use coconut oil or virgin and extra-virgin oils (any oils except nut oils) to cook with, but don't let them overheat. Any oil, when it is overheated (smoking hot and smelling strange) or reheated, will produce trans-fats which are toxic if eaten in excess. The most obvious example is fish and chips which may have been cooked in repeatedly reheated oil in a fish and chip shop. Use coconut oil sparingly, a little is excellent; too much provides an unhealthy level of saturated fatty acids.

Because our diets have radically changed in the last fifty years almost everyone is short of omega-3, the essential fatty acid which builds and repairs the membranes and nerve connections in our brains. Eating oily fish – mackerel, herring, sardines, trout and salmon – as well as a range of nuts and seeds, particularly sunflower, sesame and linseed, all of which contain omega-3, will give you and your baby all the omega-3 you need.

We digest and absorb nutrients better during the first half of the day than the second half of the day. So a slow change may be needed to make sure that you are eating a good range of fruit and vegetables at breakfast and lunch. Invent packed lunches/snacks which are really 'valuable' to replace crisps, choc bars, Coke etc. There are lots more ideas but it will depend on what you discover you like! Mashed avocado with lemon juice and pepper, mixed with sunflower seeds, pine nuts, pumpkin seeds, flaked almonds or whatever? A nut butter sandwich with a chunk of cucumber, raw carrot or tomato? Mashed potato with added spinach, broccoli or any green vegetable?

4. Nutritional supplements

People living now are the first generation coping with serious poisoning of the atmosphere, toxins in manufactured and non-organically grown food, and cleaning fluids and electromagnetic appliances in our homes. All these things are able to cause us and our unborn or young babies harm, and they can cause debilitating conditions, including depression.

Some mums might need to take nutritional supplements to 'fill the gaps' for themselves and their rapidly developing baby.

Folic acid is a daily supplement which is very important for the development of a healthy baby. It should be taken before conception (if possible) and throughout pregnancy, especially during the first twelve weeks when the spine is forming.

See www.nhs.uk to check out the foods you need to avoid during pregnancy.

5. Water

Pure, uncontaminated water has an alkaline/acid balance which regulates and balances everything in us. It also carries the nutrients we need to every cell in our bodies and washes out any toxins and poisons.

It begins a self-healing process in us when we are upset, exhausted or ill, or have hurt ourselves. It has a 'life energy' all of its own. Everyone – pregnant or not – needs to drink plenty of water, between meals, every day of their lives.

Pregnant mums need to stay away from paint thinners, paint removers, pesticides and strong cleaning agents such as bleach. The fumes are toxic, and dangerous chemicals can be absorbed by the skin.

Having looked at what we put into our bodies when we are pregnant, in the next chapter we look at ways to find peace in ourselves. This will matter just as much as what you eat and drink and how much you rest, for both you and your baby. If you feel anxious about the birth itself, the next chapter is all about finding ways to stay calm, be confident and feel loved, safe and supported.

~ CHAPTER 3 ~

What Help and Encouragement Do You Need?

NOW IT'S YOUR HEALTH AND HAPPINESS WHICH MATTER MOST!

Every mother everywhere needs to feel loved, safe and supported from the moment her pregnancy is confirmed so that her baby will feel loved and welcomed from the very beginning.

You are the bridge between your baby and the world.

Every mother deserves thoughtful attention, care and warmth from the father of her child from the moment she has her pregnancy confirmed. This will increase her confidence and hopefulness and bring both parents closer together.

Mothers who are given loving and continuing emotional, spiritual and practical support from family, friends and neighbours – and experienced advice from their midwife, community nurse and doctor – will suffer less anxiety and distress.

You will need this support even more if something serious is affecting you during your pregnancy, such as poverty, poor housing, the death of a close family member, an accident or a relationship breakdown. The support cannot be left to the chance of having family nearby or friendly neighbours, because it matters so much. When you first become pregnant, begin to think who you know well enough to trust and talk to. Try to keep in close touch with them.

Dr Joseph Chilton Pearce describes the vicious circle in which some people have become trapped:

The rising tide of violence in the world can be directly attributed to the emotional state of mothers. Right down the line, the wilder the world becomes, the wilder the emotional state of mothers. I think we have the chance to erase all forms of violence through a proper approach to pregnancy, birth and the first three years of life.
Dr Joseph Chilton Pearce
Birthlight Conference, Cambridge
July 2006

True and continuing help and support for a new family have the power to put an end to the cycle of stress and violence which is now seen in many communities. There is a much closer link than we could ever have imagined between a mother's health and feelings of happiness and security when pregnant and the effect it will have on her baby's personality and behaviour in the years to come...

... So let's first turn our attention to *you*.

PUTTING YOURSELF FIRST

Whether you are still pregnant or have already given birth, this chapter is to give you ways and ideas to help you stay calm and feel confident!

Finding and practising ways of easing stress and tension in yourself now – and as your baby grows – needs to come first. It will be crucial for the happiness of your whole family. It is like building your house on firm rock, instead of boggy ground. A house on boggy ground (life full of insecurities and uncertainties) will collapse when there are floods. When there is a drought (of love in your life), the ground will crack open and your house will tumble.

First of all, think about what your pregnancy (perhaps also the birth by now) has been like for your baby and you, and what is happening for the two of you now. What are your feelings? An up and down seesaw of happiness and anxiety? Feeling loved and protected or more and more lonely?

WAYS TO HELP YOURSELF

How can you help yourself when you feel anxious during your pregnancy, and then overwhelmed at times with the responsibility of looking after a new baby, at the same time as recovering from the birth yourself?

Thirty-five mothers, each living in very different situations, describe below their different ways of coping with stress and worry when it gets bad for them. With luck, you will find something or several things in this long list which will really help you. Whatever feels good can become a habit that is solid and real, always there to comfort you.

'I sit down or lie on my bed and I breathe deeply and slowly for at least ten breaths. As I breathe in, I silently say to myself 'Breathe in trust and hope.' As I breathe out, I silently say to myself 'Breathe out sadness and worry.' (Or any other words that make sense to me that day.)'

'I massage my forehead and stroke my eyebrows from inside to outside.'

'I listen to my own tone of voice, and try to make it warmer and more gentle. This calms me down.'

'When I feel desperate I lie in a hot bath and have just a candle on the edge for light.'

'Rubbing a hot, wet towel over my face.'

'I just get on with tidying up my toddler's mess because I know that when things get in a muddle, get lost, get broken, get in the way of cooking and mealtimes, it's impossible to feel calm.'

'Sipping a glass of water can stop me getting into a panic.'

'Looking into the distance – at the blue of the sky or the shape of the clouds or up into the greenness of a tree – helps to relax me.'

'Going out of my way to be kind to someone else usually stops me feeling upset about myself.'

'Everything I do, I try to do extra slowly, with care and gentleness – even the way I pull out the plug in the bath!'

'I sip Bach's Rescue Remedy in water. It's made from the extracts of several plants preserved in brandy and they each have something in them to make you feel calmer almost at once. I know this doesn't work for everyone but it does for me.'

'I realised that watching the TV or my computer screen for too long and the fluorescent lights in the kitchen were making me tense most of the time. I got the lights changed and started to listen to music or read a book more often.'

'I go and sit in the nearest church for five or ten minutes to think and be peaceful.'

'I put on some Latin American music and dance or just windmill my arms around for a moment or two if there's not time to dance.'

'Getting outside and planting things and weeding helps to stop me feeling fed up and worried.'

'I drink camomile tea and put a drop of lavender oil on my shirt or pillow to calm me down.'

'I phone or go and see a friend. If I neglect my friends when I get low I really am in trouble.'

'I go somewhere quiet to be alone for a few minutes and picture in my mind the loveliest place I have ever seen.'

'Stroking the back of my own hands lightly with my fingertips somehow stops my mind going round and round.'

'When I feel like screaming, I stop eating any meat for a week and eat more peas, beans, nuts, lentils, whole grains and wheat germ instead. I think it must be the extra vitamin B which helps.'

'If there are arguments starting up I get away from everyone, even for a minute if possible, to let my thoughts catch up with my emotions.'

'I try to find a calm friend to be with – not someone who's a worrier and will make it worse!'

'I listen to my own breathing for two minutes – every inch of the movement of air in and out of my lungs. The concentration calms me! Then I take four really deep breaths.'

'I say to myself "I'll feel much calmer in a minute. Just wait for it!"'

'I find that the rhythm of brushing my own or my daughter's hair gives me a calm feeling.'

'I stop trying to be perfect. Instead I try just to be myself and accept that this is the best I can do for now. That seems to deal with my miseries!'

'I just get worried thinking about the future all the time, even though it's sure to turn out different anyway! So I try to make myself live just in the present moment, as each moment comes. I practise giving all my care and attention to what I'm doing now – like the washing-up, unpacking the shopping or getting dressed. The gentleness and rhythm that comes with this concentration makes a big difference.'

'I bought a beautiful bowl and I keep it in the kitchen, often filled with fruit to eat. Every time I look at it, it gives me pleasure and eating the fruit stops the craving for sugary snack food, which I know makes me feel worse.'

'I try as often as I can to look out for things that give me pleasure: the smell of home-cooking; the feel of velvet or fleece; the movement of clouds across the sky; the sound of a bird singing even through traffic noise; the sight of long grass or corn blowing in the wind; the colours of all the different fruit and vegetables in the shops... and other people's smiles.'

'I stroke my dog or cat and I ask Ken for a hug.'

'I look at my mum's photo in the kitchen. I can hear her voice saying "Hard times always pass. Hang on in there, love!"'

'I ask my husband for help before things get even worse. I try to share everything I'm feeling as honestly as possible – without blaming him in any way. I need to know what he is feeling too, and that he understands the need for us to keep talking to each other about things that are hard, as well as when they are good, even wonderful!'

'Just as I switch off the light to go to sleep at night, thinking of one thing I feel thankful for!'

'I write down what's bugging me and then tear up the piece of paper and bin it!'

'I use the shower to calm myself down. I stand there without moving and with my eyes shut and my head tilted back a bit so the water pours over my face as well as over the rest of my body. This does a lot to wash away the misery and stress. It's the best way to help myself I ever discovered.'

You may have your own ideas to add to these? It's useful to practise your chosen calming and relaxing activities when you're feeling good about yourself and about your life because you then get into the habit of using them regularly when you need to. It's also helpful to make a list which you can look at occasionally in case you forget what has helped you in the past.

If you get worried thinking about the future all the time, even though it is sure to turn out better than you imagine, how about trying this?

Light a candle and sit in front of it. If you look at the flame steadily with unfocused eyes, you will suddenly see a beam of light coming from the candle straight towards you, like a shining pathway. Just concentrate on this beam of light and breathe gently and steadily for a moment or two. You will begin to feel calmer.

If you are new to meditation and would like to learn more, try this link to get you started:

www.mindbodygreen.com/0-42/Meditation-Techniques-for-Beginners-5-Easy-Tips.html

Also, a book which comes highly recommended is *Meditation for Beginners* by Jack Kornfield.

Right here! Right now! - Mindfulness

The word 'mindfulness' is used to mean concentration on what you are feeling, thinking, seeing with every part of your body at this exact moment. What are you doing right now? Notice your breathing, how you are sitting as you read this, and what is in your mind. The practice of mindfulness comes from the Buddhist tradition.

Whatever you are doing – even small, mundane tasks like washing a mug, pulling the plug out of the bath, putting your pants on – do it without distractions in your mind, do it slowly enough 'to watch yourself doing it' with attention and affection. Do it also with gratitude that the water is warm, the plug fits the plughole and that you have a clean pair of pants!

Being 'mindful' in this way can help us let go of stressful thoughts and feelings and help us enjoy our lives more – and our babies. Developing this thoughtfulness for the present moment, concentrating on every small task in turn, will give you the skills you need for family life. Less time will be wasted. The tensions of anxious planning ahead will quieten.

There are other skills that many people learn and use to help them steady and balance themselves. One of these is Brain Gym®.

Brain Gym® exercises

If you practise these specific physical exercises on a regular basis, they will be able to calm you, increase your brain power and memory and help your learning skills – useful achievements for anyone expecting or with a new baby!

1. Brain Buttons

Hold one hand over your navel, and with the other hand, rub quite firmly in the hollows just under your collarbone. Change your hands over, and repeat the exercise. This exercise stimulates your carotid artery which takes newly oxygenated blood to both sides of your brain simultaneously.

https://www.youtube.com/watch?v=pLpHzJCsIDw

2. Cross Crawl

March on the spot for a few minutes. As you raise your right knee, touch it with your left hand, and as you raise your left knee, touch it with your right hand. It could be fun to have some music playing while doing this, as it helps to keep your rhythm going. Children often enjoy working out some other ways of moving opposite arms and legs: stretching them out to the sides is one way. Cross Crawling is what a crawling baby does. It is a valuable part of growing up. It will do so much to balance the growth of your baby's brain. In the months ahead, the more time your baby spends crawling (and rolling), the better.

By moving opposite parts of the body at the same time, Cross Crawl helps the creative, right side of your brain and the organisational and language, left side of your brain to work together. You are helping your brain to work in a whole, switched-on way.

3. Thinking Caps

This is an exercise to get your ears ready! Hold the earlobes between your thumbs and your index fingers and roll your ears gently around about ten times. Thinking Caps makes listening, concentrating and remembering things easier. Just the act of physically stimulating receptors in the outer ear wakes up the whole hearing mechanism.

4. Lazy Eights

Here's a warm-up for your fingers and eyes. This helps with writing, sewing and any intricate work with your fingers. It is called Lazy Eights because instead of an eight being drawn upright, it is drawn lying down on its side, like the sign for infinity, . Starting at the centre, draw an eight on its side, in the air, with your finger. Go upwards first, *watching the movement of your finger all the time* as the eight shape is being made. First use one hand, then the other – then use both hands, moving side-by-side to make more Lazy Eights.

This exercise is good for your hand and eye co-ordination, and helps your eyes to track smoothly from left to right across the middle. This helps you to balance the use of your brain.

5. Hook-Ups

This exercise calms any restlessness you are feeling and helps your concentration. It is done in two parts.

Part One: Sit down, and cross one ankle over the other. Stretch out your arms and cross your wrists. Turn the palms of your hands to face each other and clasp your hands together. Now fold your clasped hands downwards, inwards and then upwards so that they rest on your chest comfortably, just underneath your chin, your elbows against your ribs. Hold in this position while you breathe deeply for a while, until you are feeling calm.

Part Two: Uncross your hands and feet, and put the tips of your fingers and thumbs together. Hold your hands like a triangular tower, in front of your neck, with arms and shoulders relaxed. Again, breathe deeply.

There are many more Brain Gym® exercises presented for adults, schoolchildren and students to watch on YouTube.

Friendship

Friendship grows out of time spent together, time talking to each other, time doing things together and through shared fun and exploration – and through the help and encouragement you give each other.

It also grows from the giving of gifts – a flower, a fruit, a lick of ice cream, a joke, a cup of tea, a plate of food, a memory, a story, the loan of a book, toys, baby clothes or bed clothes – and your own helping hands. Even tiny presents can say more than we might guess, when they are given with warmth and pleasure. They can open doors in us which may have been shut for some time. They make smiling come more easily. Smiles are easily passed on to the next person, and change the atmosphere in the room, in the shop, on the street and at any meeting place.

Look out for the happy and kind people in your community, regardless of any differences in age, what they wear or where they come from. People are people with similar needs and longings the world over. Wherever you are and whoever you meet, watch their faces and listen to the tone of their voices. If you feel drawn to anyone, find the courage to smile at them and to start a conversation. Friendliness and interest are catching. This is the first step. It is like reaching out with your mind and your heart. You won't believe what a big difference this will make to your life.

Finding friends by finding what you have in common is a good start.

> *We both love chocolate... We both watch snooker... Our children are the same age... We go to the same church, or mosque, or club, or pub... We both have a dog and they both have fleas at the moment... We both try to get out into the park each day whatever the weather.*

The next step is laughing together. Laughter often follows when strangers are suddenly brave and begin to talk openly to each other. Laughter stops you feeling shy or tense. It relaxes you and leads you on. It gives pleasure. This is how friendships grow in loyalty and lasting affection.

Learning from each other and other cultures

I learned a Zulu word from Africa – Ubuntu. This single word means 'a person is a person because of other people who care'.
A mother in Lambeth, London

I watch other mothers in the shops and in the playground and I pick out the ones who are chatting to their children and making things fun and interesting for them. I watch the way they take care of their children cheerfully, without fussing or hurrying them or shouting. I try to remember what I have seen and heard and do the same. It's hard sometimes because my mum was often bothered about things and used to shout at us and get cross easily and I find myself sometimes behaving just like her.
A mother in Putney, London

We left England a few years ago and went to live and work in Hungary, in Eastern Europe. We were stunned by the difference between what we left behind and what we found there in terms of a family-friendly life.

We left a place where neither the government nor many of the people around us seemed to believe that support of family mattered more than anything. The general attitude to children in the UK, when we look back, seems to have been uninterested, uncaring and sometimes just critical.

All over Hungary we found that the attitude to children was just the opposite. We began to relax and enjoy our baby and our three-year-old as never before. Everything just felt right and as it should be. There is courtesy and respect for grandparents and all elderly people. Neighbours and passers-by take notice of, and talk to, our children. The family comes before business and earnings.

Strangers greet each other and say 'Good day' when they part. When children greet their elders, they often say 'Csokolom' which means 'I kiss your hand'. A passer-by is always ready to help a mother struggling to get on and off the bus. There are clean parks everywhere with bright, modern playgrounds. Prams, clothes and babysitters are passed on from mother to mother on loan. Strangers stop to talk to you to admire your baby and tell you about their own children. Pregnancy is spotted at once and everyone smiles and

> *gives you help or a seat if you look as if you might need it. In public loos where there is a queue, mothers and children are always allowed to go first. The Hungarian children are given more free rein yet behave better. Parents and grandparents often move home to be near to each other. Everyone is used to and is good at handling babies and children. This 'goodness' is passed on from one generation to another.*
> **Annuska and Miklos**

Finding older friends

> *Older people, especially contented older people, are endlessly fascinating because they have 70 years of experience coiled up inside them.*
> **Doctor working to improve the hospital care of the elderly**

Parents need to have someone older who cares for them deeply, accepts them as they are, loves them and supports them.

Ben's the 'apple of her eye'

In the same way, as your baby grows up, he will need an extra grown-up who is just crazy about him. To be the 'apple of someone's eye' means a child will blossom. Sometimes, you may be too busy or too tired to spend enough time watching and listening to everything your child is trying to tell you and show you. If grandparents are too far away, it will be wonderful if your child can be 'adopted' and doted on by one of your older friends.

A welcome and support from your community

Whatever age, no one ever stops being a mother... or being a father. We need the knowledge and wisdom of motherliness and fatherliness more than anything else in our communities – perhaps more than ever before.

When parents recognise that their babies are real and complete beings in the womb, they will learn so much from them after they are born. The spirit of their newborn child will be respected and welcomed.

But what if...?

If something makes you feel continually stressed or suddenly very upset or very angry, your brain will stimulate the production of a hormone called cortisol – the 'worry' hormone. If you are pregnant, this hormone will flood your body and reach your baby through the umbilical cord. This will cause him to share your tension and misery. If this is continuous it will interfere with his healthy growth, especially his brain. He will be 'wired up' for misery and anxiety, even before he is born, unless you can change things for him.

This is the story of how one expectant mother protected her unborn baby from the grief and distress that enveloped her during her pregnancy:

> *I had a very sad and anxious time through most of my pregnancy. First, my husband became seriously ill and no one could tell me whether he would recover fully. At the same time, my dad developed cancer and was dying in hospital. For weeks I sat by his bed, holding his hand and watching him grow weaker every day. It broke my heart. I felt so upset, knowing that he would not live even to see my baby. I was holding my dad when he died.*

At the same time, I knew instinctively that all my months of anguish must, in some way, reach and perhaps harm my baby – as she was so totally part of me. What could I possibly do to protect her from the grief I was feeling?

I thought carefully and decided that I would give my baby all my loving attention whenever I was able to lie down or sit back in a comfortable chair on my own. I would stroke her, round and round, as she lay curled inside me and talk calmly and gently to her whenever I could do this – whether for just a moment, or for quite a long time.

I promised her again and again that all would be well... that the sadness would come to an end... that I would always be there to take care of her... and that we'd both be safe and happy together. I told her slowly and clearly, 'It's OK, sweetheart... it's not your fault... I'll sort it out... Don't you worry!'

I also talked out loud to her about my joy at being pregnant and how I longed for her birth and to be able to hold her in my arms. Amy was born three weeks after my dad died. I managed to talk to her and stroke her between contractions until she was born.

After she was born she was the most peaceful and contented baby possible. Within a few weeks, she was smiling away at anyone who came near her. She is now the easiest and most enchanting and loving two-year-old – and gives me such happiness and comfort.

Jo

In just the same way, whatever troubles and sadness you might be going through, you too can calm yourself for your baby's sake and for the sake of the future together.

Your own distress is real and important – and cannot be pushed aside. Yet it is still possible for you to protect your unborn baby, or your young child, by separating your fear and grief from the way you feel about your baby and how you talk to him in a calm and loving way to reassure him. He will get the message.

Find your own words. When you hear your own voice speaking slow comfort to your baby, the soothing vibrations will not only reach him but will also comfort you and help you to cope better. If you can talk to your unborn baby or young child in the same way whenever you feel full of grief, panic or anger, you will be protecting the way his brain grows and the way his personality develops.

I knew a woman who lived in the East End of London during the worst of the Blitz during World War II. Bombs rained down night after night for months on end. The noise, the fear and the sleepless nights were so continuous that when her baby son was born and grew up, he was almost unable to smile. I never heard him laugh.

Sarah, a grandmother

Some families are 'blitzed' by angry arguments and shouting, or by worries that lead to drink, drugs and breakdown. The effect on a baby, whether still in the womb, in your arms or learning to walk and talk, will be even more harmful. It will affect the way his brain grows and the way his personality develops.

A baby who is treasured and loved in the womb, whatever has happened to upset you during that time, will usually recover quickly from the birth and be happy, full of smiles and easy to look after. Your voice, your touch and keeping close day and night after his birth should also speed up his recovery if the birth itself has been hard.

Do you still need more help and support?

Perhaps you still need more practical support than is there for you and more reassurance about your pregnancy, the birth and the future? If this is so, it's really important that you ask for this help. You may be able to talk to your husband or partner, the most loved member of your family, one of your closest friends, your midwife, your health visitor or your doctor. Finding the courage to talk openly and freely about what you are feeling and asking for help may seem a big step for you. But you deserve and need support more now probably than at any other time in your life so far. All that matters is that you get it.

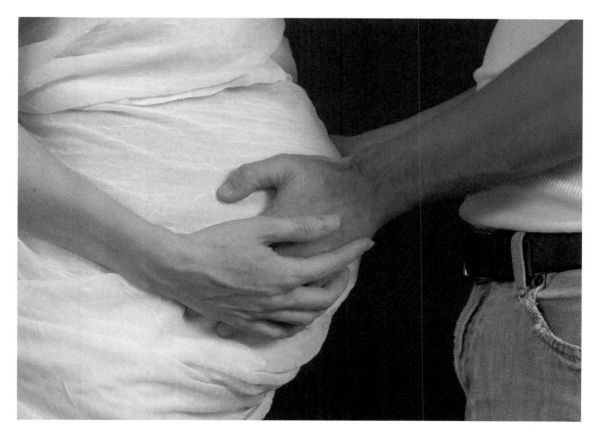

> *I believe that if every expectant mother could feel loved, comforted, protected and safe throughout pregnancy, during birth and during the early months of motherhood, the whole world could be changed in a single generation. But I don't know how on earth we can bring this about!*
> **A midwife**

Maggie Howell's natal hypnotherapy

www.natalhypnotherapy.co.uk

We warmly recommend this website for the outstanding help and support it can give you during your pregnancy and the birth of your baby. It describes for you every sort of practical step you can take to increase your sense of control and confidence, overcome fear, learn ways to reduce pain, plan for the birth with your birth partner (whoever that may be) and believe in your body and its ability to give birth.

Listening regularly to Maggie's CD, *Effective Birth Preparation, Hypnobirthing for a Hospital Birth* from when you are around thirty-two weeks pregnant could be the best possible preparation for you. You might prefer to read Maggie's book.

CDs and MP3 downloads are there to help you if you have problems with conceiving, during pregnancy, during labour or during the birth, and to help you recover from caesarean section or a long or hard birth. They also teach you lifelong stress management.

> *'I promise it works and I was sceptical! Had a bad first labour and the second, after reading this and listening to the CD, was PAINLESS! The book is so interesting and easy to read.'*
>
> *'A huge thank you for your fantastic hypnotherapy... I have just had the most amazing experience of my life!... It was a wonderful birth after such a terrible one last time... Dorothy, my midwife, kept telling me that she had never seen anyone so relaxed... I was totally able to breathe through the contractions and even managed to doze in between them... I just breathed the baby through the birth canal with one push for the head and one for the body... I was so quiet and relaxed... no one realised the baby was coming... I found it so easy to adjust and recover... my life feels just perfect. Thank you so much for teaching me your amazing skills.*
> Much love, Cathy xx'

Other mums have said:

> 'Many women do not know that they can prepare effectively for birth. For me, the key was to be confident in my ability to give birth just as millions of women had done before me and to practise relaxation techniques, so that when the time came I was able to relax my body at will. My body knew what to do, just as it knew how to grow my baby! I used the tapes for 30–35 minutes, 2 or 3 times a week during my pregnancy.'
>
> 'I learnt to "turn down" the pain through the strongest contractions.'
>
> 'The self-belief from listening to the CDs makes the birth of your baby so special.'

The next chapter encourages you to explore and turn to safe and natural remedies, from herbs, flowers and homeopathy, to help you during your pregnancy and the birth.

CHAPTER 4

How herbs, homeopathy, aromatherapy and flower remedies can help you and your baby

HERBS

Out there waiting for us are hundreds of thousands of different kinds of food growing in most corners of the world. There are also herbs and flowers able to help and heal us at particular times of need in our lives. Pregnancy is one of those times. There are five well-tried and completely safe herbs which can be very useful when we become pregnant: lime flower, lemon balm, raspberry leaf, camomile and ginger.

Lime flower

Tea made from lime flowers will calm and relax you and help you to sleep. Lime (or linden) trees grow in many places so you may be able to pick fresh lime flowers for yourself in the early summer. This tea can help to clear tension headaches and dizziness. It can also lower high blood pressure, especially if this is caused by worry. If used with lemon balm it is an excellent remedy for stress and panic.

Ginger

Ginger comes from a bulbous root called a rhizome. It is a good remedy for travel sickness, morning sickness and post-operational nausea. Eating or making a tea with about one gram of fresh ginger root can help to relieve morning sickness, at least if it is relatively mild. Ginger can also be taken as a capsule. It is also very good for improving the circulation to the hands and feet, and encourages healing of thread veins. It is an antiseptic for stomach infections like food poisoning, especially if taken with garlic. The warming and soothing effect comes quickly.

Ginger and camomile, taken together as a tea, are calming and soothing.

Raspberry leaf

Raspberry leaf tea has a direct action on the muscles of the womb during pregnancy and contains calcium which is useful for growing babies. *However, it should be taken* only *during the last three months of pregnancy and not more than one cup a day*. It helps the birth by stimulating the longitudinal muscles of the womb and relaxing the cervix. It also encourages the production of breastmilk. In between babies, it can help reduce period pains and irritable bowel discomfort.

There are other herbs that can also be helpful with different conditions during pregnancy and after the birth but you should first check them out with your doctor if you are already taking another medicine for the same condition. Just occasionally a drug can clash with a particular herbal remedy so they should not be taken together.

If you would like to find and ask a medical or master herbalist for advice, follow these links:

- www.nimh.org.uk (National Institute of Medical Herbalists)
- www.associationofmasterherbalists.co.uk
- *Herbal Remedies Handbook (Natural Care Handbook)* by Andrew Chevallier, FNIMH

HOMEOPATHY AND AROMATHERAPY

Homeopathy is a safe, simple and natural medicine for the whole family. Homeopathic remedies can help to calm you, your baby or child and to cope with sudden sickness or pain. It can be particularly valuable during pregnancy, at the birth and during babyhood and childhood because this is the time when it is important not to take painkillers, drugs or any kind of antibiotics if this can possibly be avoided.

Babies, children and animals respond very well to homeopathic remedies because their fresh and natural healing energy is so easily stimulated.

If you take homeopathic remedies when you are young, it can set you on the road to better health for the rest of your life. They can clear away inherited health problems and keep your immune system working well.

These natural remedies come mainly from a variety of plants and minerals. They work on the principle that if a particular substance would make a healthy person ill in a big dose, it will be able to cure similar symptoms of discomfort or sickness if it is given as an incredibly small dose. Exactly how homeopathy works is still a mystery. It appears to be carried by the electromagnetic energy running through our bodies and to activate healing through the water which flows through us in our blood and is in every cell. Homeopathic remedies work by stimulating our body's natural ability to heal itself.

Each remedy is developed by such repeated dilution and vigorous shaking that any originally existing toxin or poison is extinguished. The word 'homeopathy' means 'similar suffering'. For a homeopathic remedy to work its symptoms must match the symptoms of suffering. For example, a homeopathic remedy called *Allium cepa* (made from onions) is successfully used for cases of hay fever and other allergic reactions when eyes have become irritated, red and running.

Finding the right homeopathic remedy is like giving a car with a flat battery a jump-start from the battery of another car. It can give you a jump-start when you feel anxious or unwell – in your emotional self as well as your physical self. Fright, anger, grief, guilt, jealousy, even shyness and phobias, can be eased away, sometimes instantly, as well as sudden sickness and pain.

If the correct remedy is found, it will remove the cause of the problem. If the correct remedy has not been found yet, there will be no change at all but no harm done, either.

If you or your baby or child has continuing health or emotional problems, you might be glad to talk to an experienced homeopath to work out together what is going on.

Even the most serious and long-lasting conditions can often be helped by a trained homeopath. There will be a greater chance of finding the right remedy – and then maybe using one or two other remedies, in turn, to complete the healing.

Never chew or swallow the tiny pillules, but just let them dissolve in your mouth. Take them at least fifteen minutes before or fifteen minutes after eating or drinking (anything apart from water) or cleaning your teeth.

If you want to have a baby or have just become pregnant, are you feeling anxious about rubella (German measles)?

We all know how risky it is for a baby if his mother develops rubella during the first three months of pregnancy. This illness, caught by someone who has just become pregnant, can seriously damage the tiny, growing foetus.

The problem is that few of us know for certain whether or not we had this mild, flu-like disease when we were children and therefore developed an immunity to it for the rest of our lives.

If you can't remember and feel worried about this, you can ask for a rubella vaccination as soon as you decide you want a baby.

But if you prefer to avoid vaccination, the use of two homeopathic remedies, *Rubella* and *Pulsatilla*, will help to protect your baby.

If you know there is German measles in your area and you are trying to get pregnant, take *Pulsatilla 6c* twice a day for two weeks. As soon as you do conceive, take *Pulsatilla 30c*, one dose every two weeks for four months.

If you are trying to get pregnant, also take Rubella 30c every fourth day for four doses. Take four more doses as soon as you know you are pregnant.

Pregnancy and birth

Take *Ipecac*, *Nux Vomica* or *Cocullus* for 'morning sickness' during early pregnancy for heartburn later on. Try a few doses of one. If it has no effect try another.

Pulsatilla can encourage your baby to turn if it is in a breach position. This can reduce discomfort or a forceps delivery or the need for emergency intervention such as a caesarean section.

> *My baby was in the breach position a week before her birth. I took four doses of Pulsatilla and talked to her each time. I asked her if she wanted to turn round and come out head first or not. She must have picked up the message from my feelings or the tone of my voice – it's a mystery how – and she turned herself at the eleventh hour. I was so grateful she made that choice!*
> **Kathryn**

Aconite can help you to feel less anxious as you go into labour.

Caulophyllum can encourage labour to begin if you are overdue and want to avoid being induced. It can also help you if your contractions become irregular or stop and you feel shaky and anxious because there seems to be no progress for a while.

Arnica 30 (found growing high up in mountainous places), every two to four hours throughout labour, will help to prevent, also help you and your baby to recover from, any bruising, shock and distress from your labour and the birth. It reduces recovery time after childbirth, operations and accidents.

Rescue Remedy is a combination Bach flower remedy. Put a few drops in a glass of water and sip as often as you like. Alongside the *Arnica*, this can help to calm and steady you during labour.

Clary sage oil is an aromatherapy oil which can be rubbed slowly and rhythmically on your stomach and your back to reduce the ache of contractions. Three drops only in a teaspoon of olive, sunflower or almond oil.

If you have a caesarean section you will need *Arnica* first, then *Bellis Perenns* and perhaps *Staphisagria* later on to help you heal up fast.

Staphisagria will also help you if you feel upset at not having had a natural birth.

> *To have a trained homeopath within reach of every maternity ward or birth centre - with various remedies available for the different stages of labour - would be the ideal. This is beginning to happen in some places.*
> **Maggie Howell, clinical hypnotherapist and doula**

After the birth

Gelsemium can help you if you are feeling exhausted and are too tired to sleep – with your thoughts going anxiously round and round in circles.

Passiflora and *Valerian* can also help you get back to sleep quickly between night feeds.

Pulsatilla can help if you feel weepy after the birth and your emotions are in turmoil.

Ignatia can help with sadness and grief.

Bella Donna and *Phytolacca* can help with any heat and sharp pain discomfort you might briefly experience when you first start breastfeeding. They can prevent the development of mastitis.

For your baby now – and for everyone later

Any tiny homoeopathic pill can be crushed to a powder between two teaspoons and tipped into the corner of your baby's mouth. It is then like a sweet dust which immediately melts and is absorbed.

Stramonium can calm and take away the panic in a baby born with the umbilical cord around the neck.

Pulsatilla will lessen the panic in a baby who has to be separated – even for a few minutes – from his mother just after birth or in the next few hours or days; unless there is a medical emergency, avoiding such separation is critical.

Camomilla or *Calc phos* is good for older babies who are upset and screaming with the pain of teething.

Calc carb is good for young children who are stubborn and have tantrums from an early age.

Arnica is unfailingly and rapidly able to prevent as well as heal shock, bruising, bleeding, distress and fright in a child – and in anyone else in the family.

Hepar Sulph can work like a natural antibiotic.

Belladona (made from deadly nightshade) helps to bring down a high temperature.

Ledum (wild rosemary) stops a bad reaction to mosquito and other insect bites.

Nux Vomica can take away sickness and headaches.

> *Homeopathic medicines are both extremely small in dose and yet extremely powerful in their therapeutic effect.*
>
> *For 200 years now, millions of physicians and hundreds of millions of homeopathic patients have observed and experienced the power and effectiveness of homeopathic medicines.*
>
> **Dana Ullman, MPH**

- www.homeopathy-soh.org
- www.britishhomeopathic.org
- www.the-hma.org
- www.a-r-h.org/

Suppliers of homeopathic remedies:

Your local chemist or – recommended – www.ainsworths.com, www.helios.co.uk

FLOWER REMEDIES

There are many plants of every size whose flowers contain specific healing and comforting properties that have been understood and used in many parts of the world, some of them for thousands of years.

The energy (or 'vibration') of a flower can be transferred to water without including any physical part of the flower itself. The energy is drawn out of the flower or leaf by a special process, preserved in alcohol and usually given as a few drops on the tongue, administered by a dropper or else added to a little water and sipped very slowly.

Well known and much used are the *Bach Flower Remedies* – named after Dr Edward Bach. A few drops of the appropriate remedy, taken in water and held in the mouth before swallowing, are able to help relieve troubling emotions such as irritability, nervousness, sadness, suspicion, impatience, apathy – even jealousy and fearfulness. Some can also help to lift you out of depression, lost energy or a weakened immune system.

If you would like to learn more, follow this link:

www.bfvea.com (British Flower and Vibrational Essence Association)

A recommended book is *Flower Essences: An Illustrated Guide* by Carol Rudd, MA, BFVEA.

Concern is growing amongst medical researchers and doctors about the ever-reducing effectiveness of antibiotics, as well as their unpleasant side-effects. These appear to be the result of over-subscribing and the growing resistance of many harmful bacteria. In response, more hospitals, birth professionals and parents are using age-old but newly refined and more fully understood remedies from the natural world around us.

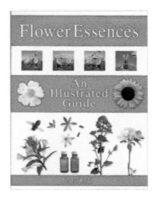

CHAPTER 5

Dads are Needed From Day One

For the majority of mothers an important ingredient for her successful pregnancy, birth and breastfeeding is the care provided by the father/partner.
Patrick M. Houser

She is having a baby. What am I supposed to be doing?

Research shows clearly how much child and family health and happiness depend on a father's involvement and sharing in his child's life from the very beginning. This includes the care he is able to give and the love he feels for his partner and for his baby at conception and right through the pregnancy.

www.fatherstobe.org/research.htm

It can be more bewildering beginning to be a dad than beginning to be a mum. Mums have no option. The experience of being pregnant, growing heavier and heavier and feeling her baby moving inside her prepares her for the life-changing birth itself – as well as what follows.

A man can only ask questions, watch and guess what's going on physically and in the thoughts and feelings of the woman carrying his child. If he had a much younger brother or sister, he may have absorbed some things about pregnancy, childbirth and the skills of baby care. If not, he could be wondering what he will be able to do to help and how he will cope with his newborn child.

> *I was lucky! From the day her pregnancy was confirmed, my wife shared her thoughts about the baby and described to me the new things she was noticing. I began to feel interested and excited. After our son was born, she encouraged me to take over and have him all to myself whenever I could. Without noticing how, I've got confidence. In a few weeks, I felt I could manage anything. That makes you proud!*
> **Dad, two months after the birth of his son**

Love for each other

Just as much as his dad's presence close by, a baby needs to sense the love between his parents during his time in the womb as well as throughout his babyhood, childhood and beyond. From the time he is born, a baby needs to see his mum and his dad looking at each other, smiling at each other and touching each other as much as he needs their smiles and touches for himself.

THE PROVIDE-AND-PROTECT INSTINCT

It seems as if there is a provide-and-protect instinct in a man's make-up especially if his own experience as a child was having a loving mum and dad, who were both there for each other and for him. This instinct has been built into men's genes, and into their muscles and brains over hundreds of thousands of years. It is strengthened by being born into a warm family who care about each other and help each other.

For a woman, there is a big difference between feeling loved and protected by the father of her child and being on her own. If she can't share with him the magic times with their baby, as well as the tough times, it's easy for her to get depressed and over-serious. She will have less lightness and love in her heart to give to a baby. As we feel loved and cherished ourselves, so we pass this love and cherishing on to our babies – and to others too.

NO DAD AROUND?

For many reasons, however, there are some women who become mothers without the father around; some even choose to get pregnant and bring up their child on their own. If something like this is the case for you, would you be able to find and invite a man you trust and feel close to, to be a regular 'stand-in dad' for your baby and through childhood? This could be your father, your brother, your brother-in-law or a very good friend who enjoys children? This will make an enormous difference to your child's future.

> *Mums and dads are different!*
>
> *I don't think many men have quite the same instinct as a woman for the minute-by-minute watchfulness, gentleness and slow-motion handling of a young baby – nor for the even more patient, watchful and endless care needed for an excitable, chaotic toddler, struggling to get to grips with everything.*
>
> *But I can't take my eyes off my grandchildren now. Love them to bits! Watching their faces and doing things with them feels so good it knocks me for six. It's as if I'm only able to be a really good 'dad' now that I'm a grandfather – with all the old work distractions out of the way and no time pressures.*
> **Granddad with eleven grandchildren**

BEING THERE FOR THE BIRTH

The Gentle Parenting website describes 'the four biggies for dads/partners at the birth'. www.gentleparenting.co.uk/kc/the-four-biggies-for-dadspartners-at-the-birth/

> *When we got to the maternity ward for the birth of our first child I was in a bad state – as worried for myself as I was for Molly. Would she be OK? Now the time had come, how was I going to manage? Suddenly I felt I'd just be in the way, in a panic and no help or comfort to her. I felt so scared I was sweating.*
>
> *A few minutes later Molly's midwife, Jane, came to talk to us. She looked straight into my face, touched my shoulder, gave me a big smile and said, 'Welcome. I'm so glad you are here too.' We sat down and she asked me lots more about what I was feeling about the birth and becoming a dad. She listened carefully. Then she explained what she might be doing to help Molly as things progressed and how I could best help Molly, and help her. She showed me where to go for a cup of tea or a bit of a stretch when I needed to. She explained to me quietly the different ways I could hold Molly and give her*

support and strength for her big effort – without talking and breaking her concentration. She also talked to me about the sense of peace and privacy Molly would need and how much it would help her, now and afterwards, to have me there during the labour. She reminded me about adrenaline and oxytocin. I began to feel completely different and ready for it all.

Every now and again – all through the labour – Jane looked up at my face and asked me how I was doing.

After our daughter was safely born and had been lying across Molly's chest for quite a long time, Jane got me to unbutton my shirt, then she picked up the tiny naked body ever so slowly and gently and gave her to me to hold against my skin. I can't tell you how big that moment was – the feel of her bareness, her warmth and her tiny movements against my skin and against my heart hit me like a bolt of lightning. You can't really describe it – it's like falling instantly in love with your own child and knowing you will want to care for her and keep her safe forever.

Jane was such a wonderful midwife and neither of us will ever forget her. Especially I'll never forget her first words to me.

A new dad

However, some fathers, for all kinds of reasons, shy away from being there at the birth of their child. Some feel that they are not yet ready for such a huge experience, especially if they've never seen anything born – not even a kitten. For some, the anxiety could be related to having had a traumatic birth themselves. Deeply buried memories of the fear and pain felt then can be stirred up years later to bring inexplicable feelings of alarm to some dads. Even the prospect of being there to watch the birth of their own child can be very distressing.

If you feel this might be so for you, understanding and support are there for you to help you heal that long-ago hurt... but you will need to talk about your feelings and ask for this help.

Practical help

> *It began to dawn on me that I had better think out the practical things that would certainly be needed from me and get my feelings sorted out and ready too – before I find myself turning into a father.*
> **Father-to-be**

- Help ensure that Mum has times in bed morning and afternoon with no interruption by visitors.
- Help ensure that Mum has regular and healthy meals and plenty of water to drink within reach.
- Plan and organise how the needs of an older child, a pet and many of the everyday jobs can be taken care of by someone else.

If you are unable, for whatever reason, to provide this protection, family and friends will be needed to take your place. They will be needed anyway for some of the time, as you can't do it all, even during paternity leave and especially if you are suffering from a shortage of sleep at night yourself.

LEARNING TOGETHER

> *My wife got so stuck into the baby she somehow couldn't bring herself to hand him over to me when he was little. I wish she had!*
> **A new dad**

Bathing, dressing and undressing, nappy-changing and baby-calming skills, are best learnt bit-by-bit together, so that there will always be two pairs of practised hands and two different but familiar voices to share the day-to-day caring, soothing and carrying. This is especially useful if Mum needs to sleep – or must attend to another child or another task. It will stop her worrying.

Talking quietly, whatever you are doing for your baby, will make everything happen more easily. The deeper sound of your voice, as you tell him what you are doing, will soon be able to calm him, even if wrestling him into his clothes is quite tricky.

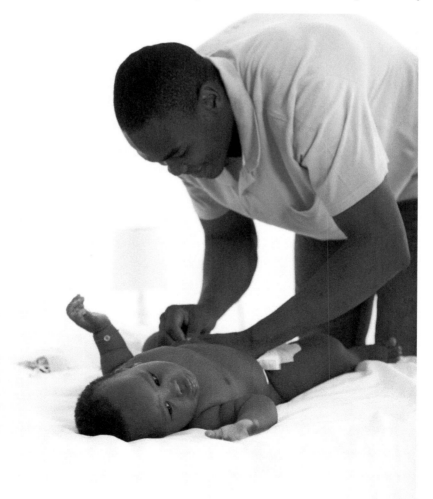

SHARING YOUR BABY

Dads learn best how to understand what is happening and what your baby is 'telling' you if you can be together to watch him closely. You will see that he is already mimicking little sounds you make and the expressions on your face. Between you, you will learn to pick up from the movements of his mouth, his eyes, his hands and his head what he is telling you without words. This will include noticing his need for little pauses of peace so he is not being overwhelmed by too much attention.

Watching together for your baby's responses and movements, you begin to realise his amazing capabilities even when he is only a few days old. This recognition of your baby's intelligence and sensitivity and his response to your smiles, your voices and your touch can be magical.

Noah Wyle describes his two-month-old son:

> *As I discover more about who my son is, I am filled with wonder and awe about how strong and intense his presence is at this early age.*

Holding and carrying a newborn baby comes more by practice than instinct. The more hours a mother and a father can spend walking about, carrying their newborn baby, the quicker it will feel really good, and the faster their confidence will grow. They will learn which positions are most calming and comfortable for their baby – perhaps vertical sometimes and horizontal at other times.

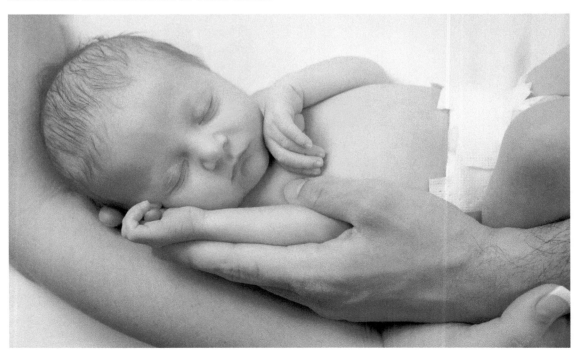

WHAT KIND OF DAD DO YOU WANT TO BE?

What was *your* dad like?

When you were little, can you remember your own dad holding you, cuddling you, bathing you, chatting with you, telling you stories, playing games with you, teaching you to walk, kick balls, jump puddles and having other kinds of fun together? If you missed out on much of this, you could now be feeling uncomfortable and uncertain about how to begin being a dad yourself. First, sit and think about what you wish you could have experienced, tried out and enjoyed with a grown-up when you were very young. You might have a close friend who you see is a good dad – loving and playing with his children – who you could watch and talk to?

When a father is around during pregnancy, when both parents are sleeping in the same bed, eating together, walking, talking and laughing together – their baby in the womb gets these messages as indelible sensations. He will be building up a sense of being surrounded by love and close to the man who gave him his life – his dad.

For every dad it's different!

> *'I want to feel that Katie's carrying our baby and that I am carrying our family.'*
>
> *'I don't want to be on the outside looking in. I don't want to be a bystander. I want to be right there in the thick of things - though perhaps not the dirty nappies!'*
>
> *'It's the money that counts. If you have to work long hours - or travel miles from home to keep your family afloat - you aren't gonna have the energy to help with a new baby. Sometimes I feel angry, sometimes I feel relieved.'*
>
> *'When our baby was newborn and was crying and that, her dad just went off and played with the dog! I had to wait for weeks to get him to hold her, even for a short time, and a bit later to take her out to show her things in the garden. Now he adores her and she goes crazy the moment she sees him walk into the room.'*

Life is changing

Recently, in western cultures, more dads are there at the birth of their baby than ever before. They are also getting involved in all kinds of baby and toddler care – feeding, buggy-pushing, shopping, bath-time, storytelling and so on. As his baby gets older, it seems as if a larger amount of a dad's time with his children is spent in games and playing.

The powerful instinct to care and protect babies and young children is ready and waiting from a very young age. If they feel loved and secure themselves, even very young boys show tenderness and competence with a baby entrusted to them. This also shows strongly in most teenage boys whenever they are trusted to care for a baby or young child, without any pressure to make them feel self-conscious.

Questions to ask yourself before your baby is born
- What ideas and hopes about fathering do you have?
- In what ways do you think you will be able try to help your family be happy and close?
- How much time will you give your children each day?
- How much do you think mothering and fathering should overlap?
- What sort of overlap do you both want – and when?
- When and how will you – Dad and Mum – try to make time for each other?
- What better support do you feel you need?

Boys who had a 'lonely' babyhood and stressed childhood might have very different emotions when they become fathers:

> *I'm apprehensive about being a father because I might find myself being like my dad was to us - what he did to us. Somehow I'll have to unlearn the way he was with us and try to do the opposite. I can't face being that way – I can't face repeating the disapproving way he treated us. I'll learn different. I'll keep telling myself 'That's good!' 'That's OK!'*
> **Damien**

Two expectant dads talking together during a break from work

A dad is very important to his baby

Here is a story from the wife of a teacher:

> *I became pregnant with our first child just as my husband got a new, very demanding job. Towards the end of my pregnancy he was off to work very early and often not home until 9pm or later – by which time I was asleep in bed.*
>
> *During that time, a close friend of ours, Brian – who had been my husband's best man at our wedding – came to live with us. He had been made redundant and was trying to find a new job in a bigger city. He was in and out of the house and helping me for a good part of most days. So we were talking together on and off during the last few months before the baby was born.*
>
> *What shocked us all from the day Pete was born was that whenever Brian held him in his arms and talked to him he was immediately soothed and lay contentedly, staring at his face and listening to his voice as if recognising an old friend. In contrast, whenever his own dad held him and talked to him during that first month he struggled and would often cry and look away. My husband's voice was not nearly as familiar to him as Brian's voice and he was therefore much less able to calm Pete and make him feel safe in those early weeks.*

Luckily the school holidays started just then so Pete could get tuned in to his own dad's voice and soon came to feel happy in his arms too. We all joked about it but it had been quite upsetting at the time because we had no idea that such a thing could happen.

If the world could be as ideal as we can make it, every baby would have a dad or at least a loving uncle or granddad within close reach... or a new live-in boyfriend of his mum's who cares about him as if he was his own son.

Handling a newborn baby

It needs first courage and then practice for a dad to learn to relax and handle his newborn baby tenderly and easily. If he is feeling helpless in the face of this looming responsibility, it may be harder for him to get stuck in. For example, one of the first undertakings for a dad may be to guard them both from a rush of visits from other family members and friends... as well as to share the holding and soothing of a sometimes crying and struggling bundle.

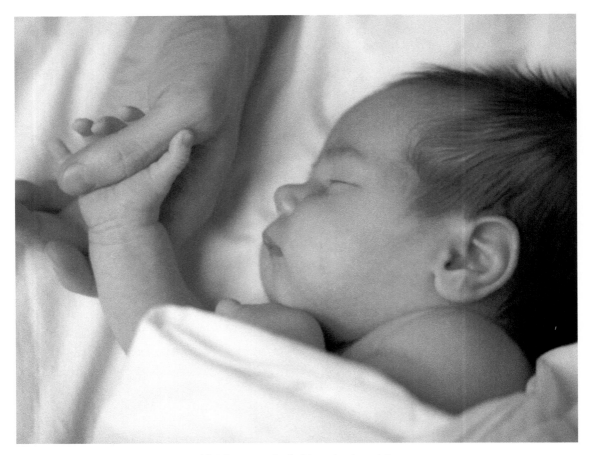

Holding my dad's thumb already!

Take charge!

All new mums need someone to make sure they have hours of peaceful time every day with their baby. Only this way can they get totally absorbed with their baby, which is how it is meant to be. This will also help them to recover as quickly as possible from the birth and to feel more secure and calm with each other as the days go by. A lifelong bond will develop between you all. This is where dads can help most.

Visitors don't necessarily think of this, not knowing how many other people have already come to see the new arrival that day. They may follow, one after another, in a celebratory stream. The excitement of it can be unforgettable but the wear and tear can kick in too and be exhausting and upsetting.

Planning the day together

As part of the need to protect Mum and baby in the early weeks, is it possible to plan a framework for the day?

Special differences

What a child learns from his mother and what he learns from his father – how he is helped in all kinds of ways – will be different. This is just how every baby needs it to be.

Sometimes, Dad's deeper and slower voice creates vibrations which can calm his newborn baby who is crying with the strangeness of life after birth.

Later on, Dad's rough-and-tumble play on the ground with an older child will instinctively show him physical controls and skills and the important dividing line between fun and mock aggression – and violence that hurts. Few mums have this built-in skill.

The differences in personality and role can be very helpful to the baby in his development. If, as far as possible, Mum and Dad can embrace their differences this will be very helpful.

Got yer!!

Teamwork

Although it's ideal and wonderful for the family to be with each other as much as possible during the pregnancy, the birth and babyhood, there is and always will be the strong (thousands-of-years-old) instinct and practice for mothers to stay closest to their baby day and night to feed and nurture them as needed. The instinct and habit has been for fathers to work as best they can to care for their new family and to provide food, warmth, shelter and protection. This is based on ancient human need and common sense.

The biggest and toughest challenge for a dad now, maybe, is how to protect and provide for his family at times when unemployment, unpaid bills and housing problems bring feelings of anger and helplessness.

> *When a man works to provide for a woman – even at lean and difficult times – and protects her, especially during her pregnancy and the years when her children are young and vulnerable, he's doing a Great Good!*
> **A health visitor**

Love your husband or partner with all you have

Dads need support from all sides, too. What times could you somehow find to sit close and give each other your loving attention and smiles – even with a newborn baby and your head full of thoughts of the birth and the next feed?

Research tells us that boys are more vulnerable than girls to the effects of their father's emotional and mental health.

♥ Babies whose fathers feel left out and become silently depressed during the first weeks after birth are more likely to develop behaviour and emotional problems themselves later.

♥ Children whose fathers are alcoholic or are on drugs are more likely to suffer from mood disorders, depression and get hooked on drink and drugs themselves when they are older.

New dads need other dads to look out for them and get them talking, cooking, digging and into their favourite sport.

What do you feel about all this? Does it make sense to you? Even just talking about things which are troubling can lift some of the burden.

Faith, hope and love

Helping each other hold onto these great human qualities, regardless of big practical worries and hardship will help you to think your way through the turmoil and to find ways, bit by bit, to reduce the problems.

What research tells us

Research across the world shows the goodness of the impact of Dad's involvement.

- Breastfeeding is more successful and goes on longer.
- 'Baby blues' and postnatal depression are less likely.
- Babies grow into children who tend to be happy and confident – ready to be kind, make friends easily and learn well in school.
- Children with the attention of involved and devoted fathers are very much less likely to be drawn into crime, drugs and alcohol abuse, or gang violence.

Dad on his own

Sometimes a dad is left to be both Mum and Dad to his child. For example, more than 400,000 families in the UK in 2012 were 'lone father families' and the numbers continue to grow. Some had help in caring for their young children, some had none. This can be a tough and huge responsibility.

The rising tide

There's a rising tide of support and encouragement for dads – especially for lone dads – available now through organisations like the Fatherhood Institute, Fathers To Be, the NSPCC and other childcare organisations.

The Fatherhood Institute – www.fatherhoodinstitute.org – publishes a free email newsletter. Expectant dads can sign up to receive monthly emails giving useful information about each month of the developing pregnancy. It sets up courses and conferences for fathers. It also works to ensure that support for fathers is fully included in government family policy. Associated with the Fatherhood Institute is a free information service for dads, www.dad.info. Dad.info distributes Dad Guides, Dad Packs and Dad Cards.

A Dad Card is an information card offering advice on everything from how dads can help out at the birth to coping with postnatal depression. The Royal College of Midwives has recommended that free Dad Cards should be available to every new father in the UK. Better information for dads can really help both mother and baby to thrive. Dad Cards aimed at Muslim, African Caribbean, Bengali, Somali and French-speaking West African dads are also available.

There is a second card, the Early Years Dad Card, for dads with toddlers and young children. All cards are available through children's centres, other early-year services and through mailings@fatherhoodinstitute.org.

I'm saying 'Hi' and talking to my new brother!

Fathers To Be – www.fatherstobe.org – gives expectant and new dads confidence by warming and deepening their understanding and their feelings for their partner and their baby. It also supports them in their relationship with the healthcare professionals caring for the family. It offers excellent preparation for fatherhood through practical education. All this can help families to grow strong and to stay together.

The *Fathers-To-Be Handbook: A Road Map for the Transition to Fatherhood* is by Patrick Houser. As Patrick says, like any map, the *Fathers-To-Be Handbook* will give you many possible routes to follow – and tools to use – to help you get to where you would like to be, as a loving father to your children and contributor to your family.

This book is also for mums, grandparents and birth professionals to read.

There is a Fathers-To-Be shop with DVDs and other helpful tools, and also a blog forum so that dads, anywhere in the world, can share their experiences and discoveries with each other.

In Sweden dads have three months of mandatory, paid paternity leave. This makes a big difference to family peace and stability.

Extraordinary new discoveries

You will find in the next chapter, 'Your Brain and Your Heart', some extraordinary new discoveries about the way our brains develop before and after birth, and the non-stop 'conversation' between our heart and brain. This new knowledge is invaluable to every one of us. It can help us to understand our unborn and newborn babies more fully than ever before, and respond to them in ways which can transform the rest of their lives – and our own.

All these neurological and medical discoveries confirm what has been known instinctively by many people for thousands of years.

~ CHAPTER 6 ~

Your Brain and your Heart

We can't run fast like a hunting leopard and we don't have claws so, over hundreds of thousands of years, we developed big skulls and amazing brains to survive. This could only happen because we ate all kinds of protein – meat, fish, nuts and seeds.

In this chapter we have reduced the enormous complexities of recent scientific discoveries about a child's growing brain to simple details. We only include here valuable knowledge and understanding about the growth of the three main parts of a baby's brain. We describe the web of connections building at great speed between all the brain cells.

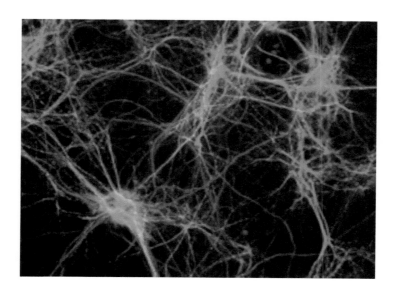

We explore the amazing new discoveries about the working link between the brain and heart. We also describe the power of a mother's electromagnetic energy to encircle and protect her baby or child. We only paint a picture here of what stands out as being of the greatest importance for every parent to know about and to understand – as well as anyone else helping to care for your child.

YOUR BABY'S BRAIN AND HOW IT DEVELOPS

The experiences that begin to fire and wire your baby's brain start in the womb, soon after conception. Our knowledge about this continues to leap forward.

Since 1965, new medical technology – ultrasound imaging, fibre optics, scanning and electron microscopes – has allowed us for the first time to photograph, test and watch a baby in the womb. We can watch every step of his development, particularly his brain development, and we can see something of his individual habits, his behaviour and his responses to what is going on in his mother's life, including what she is eating and drinking, and whether she is smoking or not.

We are now, for the first time, discovering the extent of a baby's growing intelligence, sensitivity and 'memory', especially during the last few months in the womb. We now know how much we have, in the past, underestimated every unborn baby's talents and understanding. Before a baby is born he is a real person, able to taste, hear, learn, move at will and sense each moment what is going on in his mother's heart and mind. He will remember those sensations and feelings in every cell in his body.

Not long after conception a baby's brain begins to grow at lightning speed and continues at a great pace from birth and throughout the first two years of life. A baby's brain more than doubles its weight in the first year. Later in childhood, brain growth slows a little. This first and biggest surge in growth is more or less complete, with most of the important connections in place by the age of seven.

There is an important connection between the love and cherishing enveloping a baby, before, during and after birth – and the healthy and happy completion of this rapid, early brain growth.

Last year, when I was nearly five months pregnant I opened a journal that was lying there, in the dentist's waiting room. There was an article in it that really woke me up.

It showed loads of evidence about a baby's need to be loved – you know, really treasured – by its mum and its dad in the womb as well as after its birth. It described how the 'feeling' part of a baby's brain can't develop properly if there's no love and devotion in these early stages.

I felt really shocked because there I was, carrying on at work for as long as possible and too distracted to give more than a passing thought to my baby. He was just 'my bump', getting bigger each week. I never thought that he needed my loving attention until after he was born.

Reading that article really jolted me. It showed that by neglecting my baby I had been harming both of us. From that day I began talking and singing to him at quiet moments so he could begin to hear the love in my voice. I got in the habit of stroking him and holding my open hands around my belly. Sometimes I just sat and pictured how wonderful it was going to be when I could hold him in my arms and he would see my face! He was no longer just 'a bump' to me. I began to feel that we already knew and loved each other. I sensed that this would help both of us through the birth and also as we settled down together afterwards.

A mum with a new baby

Brain research

Since 1998, huge new discoveries have been made by brain researchers and scientists across the world about how the different parts of our brain grow, from the time we are conceived. This work has been distilled and given to us by such pioneers as Dr Joseph Chilton Pearce, Jaak Panksepp, Allan Schore and Joseph LeDoux. Their research now shows us how each part of the brain develops and works in thousands of different ways, connecting with each other in incredibly intricate and complex patterns. All these 'goings-on' are being watched and understood now as never before.

One of the first things that this scientific evidence shows us is that a mother's emotions during her pregnancy and during the first year after birth have the greatest influence of all on the balanced and healthy development of her baby's brain.

Feeling calm, steady and hopeful during pregnancy can matter just as much for her baby as what a mother eats. To understand how a mother's emotions can affect her unborn baby for the rest of his life, we first need to know something of the way human brains have developed over millions of years.

This is how it all happened...

Our reptilian brain

The oldest part of our brain has been there since human time began. It is the brain we share with birds, reptiles and every other living animal. This ancient reptilian brain is like a swelling at the top of the spinal cord. It deals with the basics: hunger, temperature control, defending our 'patch' or our possessions, the urge to reproduce and to protect ourselves and our children. It's there to help us survive and to stay alive by going into the attack or by running away and hiding. It's automatic. You can't reason with it or argue with it. Our reptilian brain cannot think. It can only act and react but it *can* be influenced – it can be calmed down – through the wisdom and experience reaching and influencing it from other parts of our brain.

The thing about this early brain that has been there forever is that you don't try to reason with it nor argue with it. Before you are old enough to think you just do what it tells you immediately and without question.

Frustration and panic

Our mammalian brain

Our much bigger, mammalian brain fills our skull. It is extremely busy with thoughts, feelings, emotions and moods – all affecting our hormones and our behaviour.

The mammalian brain developed slowly over hundreds of thousands of years – much later than the reptilian brain which had been with us forever. We share this brain with other mammals like dogs, cats and horses, and even mice – but ours is a great deal larger and with much more potential.

You only need to compare the head of a lizard and of a dog to recognise the difference between a reptilian brain and a mammalian brain. Our huge mammalian brain works overtime to sort out our thoughts, emotions, ideas and plans. It replays again and again our experiences from the past, possibilities for our future and our likes and dislikes. The mammalian brain is also involved in the working of our immune system because our health and wellbeing are closely connected to our emotions.

The brain is therefore very involved with parental love and care, with playfulness, with talking to each other and with all communication sounds and signs – laughter, shouting, sighing, singing, crying, also facial expressions and all other kinds of body language.

Rapidly growing prefrontal cortex of a happy, well-loved child

The birth of our prefrontal cortex (sometimes called the neocortex)

A gigantic leap forward took place around 40,000 years ago when an entirely new part of the mammalian brain, the prefrontal cortex, began to develop for the first time. It has increased in size over the centuries. The prefrontal cortex lies in the forehead, just behind our eyes. It is sometimes called 'the social brain' or 'the third eye' (of love and wisdom).

The prefrontal cortex is the part of the brain which ties us in with our family, our community and our culture. It only starts to grow in great leaps after birth when a baby first sees his mother's smiling face and feels her gentle touch. Its full growth will truly depend on the degree of closeness and tenderness between mother and baby and their growing delight in each other.

Shining eye contact, smiles, quiet talk, being 'in arms' or within arm's reach day and night for at least the first six months – this has a startling effect on the growth of the prefrontal cortex. The continuous close presence of a mother who is calm and confident – or a one-to-one, loving and familiar mother figure there in her stead – lies at the heart of all good things to follow in every child's life.

The prefrontal cortex is sometimes referred to as our 'angel lobes' because of the love, compassion, empathy, understanding, advanced intellectual skills and language development that are centred here. It can watch over and influence all the other parts of the brain. It can even calm down and control the unthinking, self-centred reactions of the reptilian brain.

The prefrontal cortex is the only part of the brain that does not begin to grow until after birth, yet its growth is so rapid in a well-loved baby, that it is virtually completed during the first two years of a child's life – with final growth spurts at some time during puberty and between eighteen and twenty-one years.

Every time you lovingly touch your baby's skin,
thousands of new brain cells leap into life

GROWTH SPURTS IN YOUR BABY'S BRAIN

When I first got pregnant, I sat around most of the time at work, watching telly or talking to friends. I didn't move much, except to clean the flat and shop. Before my second pregnancy, I learned how much unborn babies enjoy and need lots of movement to give them the stimulation and plenty of oxygen for their growth – especially the growth of their brains. So, once I was three months pregnant, I got walking every day – jogging for a minute or two now and again while I walked – before I got too heavy! I danced around to my favourite music and sometimes I managed to go swimming.
Maggie

Physical and emotional human development comes in spurts. There are quite clear stages in a baby's brain development during the time in the womb: the first nine months after birth, especially between six and eight months; the last three months before a baby reaches his first birthday; and from twelve to twenty months.

1. Still in the womb

This is the time when the two main parts of the brain are developing, the reptilian and the mammalian, and all the nerve connections are growing between them to link sight, hearing, skin and all the new muscles growing and being tested whenever your baby is awake.

The success of this early brain and nerve development will depend to a great extent on how much a baby is beginning to sense being loved and welcomed by his parents, other members of the family and close friends. Being talked to, sung to, stroked and touched through the mother's belly will have a stronger and stronger effect throughout the nine months in the womb.

2. Birth to nine months

The first sight of his mother's smiling face, her smell, her touch and her voice – and his dad's voice – will be the spark which ignites the growth of his prefrontal cortex. It will start to grow from that moment. The baby is watching, listening, experiencing and learning so many new things every single day that his brain cells and brain cell connections are multiplying faster and faster. Every time his skin is lovingly touched, thousands of new brain cells leap into life! It is easy to see the speed of his brain development before our eyes.

3. From six to eight months

During this time, babies often develop an intense concentration on their mother's face and listening to her voice – and in their dad's face and voice.

Their rapidly growing intelligence makes them long to work out what their parents are feeling and how these feelings may change.

4. From nine to twelve months

It is in this short period that the prefrontal cortex has a massive growth spurt to connect up with the rest of the brain and begin to bring everything into a working balance and harmony. The prefrontal cortex is largely in place now. If your baby has been wanted and loved tenderly during the pregnancy he will be able, more and more, to show his love for you.

On the other hand, if the birth has been really scary and painful for him, it may take some time for him to recover and *feel* wanted and loved. He will need even more closeness and loving touch to recover.

The prefrontal cortex with all its human qualities – and its link with the heart – will then lead the way for the rest of that child's life.

5. From twelve to twenty months

Whatever problems a toddler causes you at this stage, he needs to be nurtured with unending love, patience and comforting because these are the months in his life when all the parts of his brain are now connecting and in action all the time. It is this love and patience that helps the prefrontal cortex to grow fully. This means that your child's brain will, for the first time, be functioning as a working whole.

This means that you *must* have the help and the support you need not to feel alone and find yourself growing desperate.

Older babies and toddlers who are ignored, pushed about, smacked or shouted at, for whatever reason, will be in big trouble. The prefrontal cortex will not grow fully and connect up with the rest of the brain. Instead, the emotional part of the mammalian brain and the ancient reptilian survival brain will take over in self-protection. These children's instinctively kind, affectionate and generous nature will be less and less able to flower.

Thinking ahead

There are further brain growth spurts throughout childhood, even up to twenty-five years old. During puberty and early adulthood, when the prefrontal cortex is undergoing a final spurt of growth, the brain is in a very malleable state. These growth spurts are deeply influenced by forces for good, the love and trust between you and your child, playing, creating and exploring together, neighbourly kindness and support, involvement in community projects, involvement in the work of charities caring for families.

These growth spurts are also deeply influenced by forces for evil such as loneliness, neglect, abuse and depression at home, bullying, street and screen violence and all that visually brings death and destruction, suicide bombing and killings for a distorted cause close to home.

THERE IS ALSO A BRAIN IN YOUR HEART!

The heart is profoundly more than a pump. We must allow the heart to teach us a new way of thinking.
Rudolf Steiner

For many people, this is a strange new thought. It's hard to believe, but your heart is much more than a pump sending blood around almost fifteen miles of your arteries and veins. There is also a 'brain' in your heart which is connected to, and works closely with, the brain cells in your head, in the prefrontal cortex.

At least half of the cells in your heart muscles are neural cells just like those in your brain. Millions of them have now been painstakingly counted by brain research teams, as have other small clusters of brain cells in other parts of the body. Through a mass of nerve and electromagnetic connections, there is a direct pathway between the prefrontal cortex and the neurons in your heart. The prefrontal cortex, working closely with the brain cells in our heart, enables us to understand and empathise with other people's feelings. This working together of our two 'brains' helps us to grow kind, loving, generous and wise, as well as humorous. And able to build warm, trusting and lasting relationships. What it does for us is magical!

> *Neural-cardiology is the name for the scientific investigation into the working partnership between our brain and our heart.*

Brain-heart communication

Did you know that the millions of brain cells in the muscles of your heart are 'talking' to the brain cells in your head? Your heart, as well as being a non-stop pump, is active in other ways. Nurturing, loving, spiritual understanding and wisdom come from your heart directly into the emotional part of your brain and your thinking, and therefore give you the best help of all when you become parents.

Your heart feels, senses, learns and remembers what is going on in your life, and this is passed on to your brain. This 'conversation' going on between your brain and the intelligence in your heart continues even when you are asleep.

All over the world, most people know intuitively that their hearts are much more than a bunch of continuously working muscles. We show this understanding in the words we use when we talk to each other, as well as in writings down the ages. We describe each other as being 'warm hearted', 'big hearted', a 'sweetheart', 'heart-broken', 'hard hearted', 'downhearted', 'heartless', 'heavy hearted', 'soft hearted' and so on.

We talk about 'putting our whole heart and soul' into something we are doing.

Some people talk about 'seeing through the eye of the heart'. This is in recognition that there is a spiritual energy and unity between all people and all living things in creation.

This goes on in every different language, all over the world!

Until very recently we have only known instinctively that there is 'intelligence' in our heart. Now our instincts have been backed up by a science called 'neuroradiology'. But many people never give a thought to the brain in their heart, even if they do notice the feelings in their heart and how they seem to connect somehow with the thoughts in their head.

Research by Christopher Walsh MD, PhD, Professor of Paediatrics and Neurology at the Boston Children's Hospital, shows us that the neurons in the prefrontal cortex are a closer match to the neurons in the heart than to most of those in the rest of the brain.

The HeartMath Institute, drawing from heart research from around the world and using scanning and imaging devices, tells us how your heart 'talks' to your brain through your nervous system, your electromagnetic energy, your pulse and your hormones. www.heartmath.org

Your heart-brain acts independently of your head-brain to learn, remember, make decisions, feel and sense. Indeed, your heart sends more information to your brain than the brain sends to your heart.

The intelligence in your heart can guide the intelligence in your head. When we understand this and allow it to happen, there will be less need or room for unkindness, cruel behaviour and the ancient survival strategies of fighting back, hiding away or fleeing in panic.

When we give birth and start to build a family, we may need the wisdom, love and common sense in our hearts more than at any other time in our lives.

Heart-to-heart communication

When the heart-brain connection is strong – because of the growing tenderness and understanding between mother and child – something else happens as well: a direct heart-to-heart communication between them (bypassing the brain!) will be there too. This means that a mother's smiles, gentle touch and comforting talk will help to heal a baby or child who has had a hard birth or is not well. This direct heart-to-heart communication and healing can also take place between a human being and a much-loved pet.

Feeling loved really matters to mums!

Women who have felt loved, protected, safe throughout their pregnancy will give birth to a baby whose brain development has not faltered. This feeling of security and happiness in every expectant mother matters so much because it will feed through to the baby she is carrying in her womb – just when different parts of his brain are growing incredibly fast and connecting up for the first time.

This astonishing growth continues after birth. A baby's brain will triple in weight in the first three years of life with about 1,000 trillion connections. It is loving and steady parenting that protects this growth.

Because of all we now know about brain growth, protecting and loving care of every woman who is expecting a baby should become a big priority everywhere in the world – even, somehow, in the midst of social and political unrest. Some of the poorest and most deprived families in the world often show a greater level of care for their babies and young children than those living in wealth and comfort.

If a woman, once she is pregnant, knows that the people around her support her, honour her and her pregnancy, and are ready to give her unstinting comfort, encouragement and help, she will never feel alone nor despairing.

A big danger

When a mother-to-be is considerably stressed, anxious, fearful or angry for periods of time during her pregnancy, the brain development of her baby will almost certainly be affected. Her unborn (and newborn) baby will pick up these stresses directly from her. The stress chemicals and hormones from her brain will be circulating round her body and will reach her baby through the umbilical cord. The message that reaches her baby is of fear and uncertainty. The effect of this is that his reptilian brain – the survival part of his brain – will grow larger, and his mammalian brain – the thinking, feeling part – will be unable to develop as fully and well as it should.

The question for a baby in the womb is, 'Can I go for more intelligence or must I do nothing but defend myself from the scary, worrying atmosphere I find myself in?'
Joseph Chilton Pearce

Feeling loved really matters to unborn and newborn babies

The very moment a newborn baby sees his mother's face – her smile and her shining eyes – and feels her hands gently holding and stroking him... and smells her smell... and hears the voice clearly which he already knows from the womb – his prefrontal cortex begins to grow in leaps and bounds. This growth will entirely depend, from his birth and throughout the next two years, on the continuous loving bond and tender communication between mother and baby. It will also depend on the gentle care and the smiles of everyone else who helps to look after him, especially his own father and, if he is lucky, his grandparents, during the first few years of his life.

There is a massive burst of new brain connections being made in the prefrontal cortex of a baby between six and nine months old. This is because it is often the time when pleasure and delight in your baby can be most intense and the attachment between you grows stronger every day. Another very big spurt of growth of these brain connections comes in early toddlerhood when the excitement of being able to move independently creates elation in your child and pride and joy in you. And this extraordinary brain growth continues to surge for the next seven years.

> *To experience a warm world inside your head depends very much on special one-to-one moments with your parents.*
>
> *Particular ways of responding to your young child will establish pathways in his brain to enable him to manage emotions, to think rationally under pressure and calm himself down without recourse to angry outbursts, attacks of anxiety or, in later life, alcohol, smoking and drugs.*
> **Margot Sunderland, Child Psychologist and Psychotherapist**

It is through the millions of connections in the prefrontal cortex that we discover feelings in ourselves of tenderness, kindness, empathy, devotion, compassion, trust, respect, joy, delight, fun, loyalty, patience, generosity and intimacy ('into me see'). The list goes on and we can recognise these human qualities in the behaviour of people around us, if we watch out for them.

With the final and full growth later of a child's prefrontal cortex, it will become the 'master brain'. The thoughts and emotions – particularly hard-to-bear buried thoughts and feelings – in his mammalian brain, as well as any panic reactions from his reptilian brain can be calmed and regulated.

It is also through the nearly complete growth of the prefrontal cortex in earliest childhood that we become able to explore, feel and grow in understanding of the spiritual energy in our lives and in the world around us.

Women who are naturally calm and have a deep sense of the spirit create their own environment of acceptance, expectation, feelings of safety and joyfulness. They will not need so much support from outside to ensure the whole and complete growth of their baby's brain.

The first thing a newborn baby does...

> *Most of the critical times for brain development appear to come before the age of six months.*
>
> **Pam Linke, researcher and author of books on parenting skills and infant mental health in Australia**

The first thing a baby does, as soon as he is born, is to search for his mother's face and try with all his energy to focus on it. He also turns his head towards familiar voices, especially his mother's which he knows so well. From this moment, his mother's and his father's loving looks, smiles and voices will have a very big effect on the development of his brain. A joyful welcome, tender touch, his mother's smiles day after day, are what will ensure the development of her baby's prefrontal cortex. This will also lead to the growth of more and more connections between the different parts of his brain. A baby's continuous experience of unchanging love and care – or times of uncertainty, loneliness and neglect – affects not only the number of brain cells which will develop and the connections between them, but also the way these connections are 'wired'.

Where do our emotions come from?

Every emotion we feel comes directly from the experiences we had in the past or are having now. The memory of those experiences and emotions is still with us, even if they were so far back in our lives we no longer remember them consciously. Our body often responds to strong emotions – be they happy or sad ones – just before our minds do. First, we feel the physical sensations – perhaps our heart beats faster, or our face lights up, or we feel tense, or hot and sweaty, or shivery, or numb, or we clench some muscles. Almost the moment this physical response begins in us, we feel a surge of emotion, whether this is happiness, excitement, confusion, frustration, jealousy, fear, anger, or the loneliness of being abandoned. Sometimes it might be several of these in quick succession.

> *In Sweden, parents are taught that snuggling your baby for the first 18 months is the only answer. A crib or cot at any distance from your bed at night, the use of a play pen, leaving a baby or toddler to watch television or strapped in a push chair where he can't even see you – to keep him quiet or to free you for something else – prevent the baby's healthy brain development. There is encouragement all the way to help parents, especially mothers, to understand why this is so.*
>
> **Dr Joseph Chilton Pearce**

When there is a balanced wholeness in a child's brain, and a strong brain-heart connection, that child will be able to grow up imaginative, creative and happy. Those three characteristics lead to sensitivity and an interest in everything and everyone. This, in turn, will encourage understanding and kindness towards others.

Children with a rich imagination cannot become violent and cannot be drawn into violence. They will be able to see other ways of responding and want to do so.

Margot Sunderland describes how stress and helplessness in parents sculpt the brain of their child. It can set off a ripple of hormonal changes that permanently wire a child's brain to cope with a malevolent world. Through this chain of events, violence and abuse are passed from generation to generation as well as from one society to the next. The lack of respect for a child's personal dignity and the fear and unkindnesses that they have to bear will mean that we shall continue to have terrible wars in the family, in the local community and between the nations of the world. Margot is passionate about achieving social change for a kinder, warmer world.

YOUR HEART AND ELECTROMAGNETIC ENERGY

A mother's heart is like the sun

In photographs we can see streamers of light, heat and energy flowing and circling hundreds of miles out from the sun's surface. These streamers are explosions of electromagnetic energy.

The earth has the same patterns of energy, without the violence of the sun. This is called the 'magnetic field' and this moves invisibly through the earth and around and above its surface. Lines of electromagnetic force arc out from the north and south poles around the earth in just the same way as your heart's electromagnetic field does around your body.

Every living creature has its own magnetic field and that includes every one of us. It is the three separate phases of the beat of a heart that cause the electromagnetic field in and around the heart.

It is now possible to take an image of a living heart showing the electromagnetic energies as a three-fold wave of circling 'threads' reaching out from and returning to the heart. This 'wave field' circling through and around us carries knowledge and understanding of the world – far more than has ever been fed into our heart by our brain.

When we go into thoughts and feelings which are negative, we are in defensive mode. The signals we are giving out through the electromagnetic energy from our heart can be picked up way outside the body as well as around the heart. These electromagnetic frequencies are like an energy that keeps going on and on in and around us.

When we come to understand this we are able to listen to our heart and learn a better way to live and to take care of each other and especially our newborn babies.

The connection between a mother's heart and her baby's heart

Your electromagnetic energy arcs are very strong for the first three feet. They completely encircle a baby in your arms, in a sling, or sleeping close to you at night. It is this energy from your heart which will help to protect and strengthen a newborn baby.

We now know for sure that these energy waves coming from the heart are sixty times stronger than the energy waves produced by the brain. This could mean that the feelings of our heart are sixty times more important to us as parents and to our baby than the thoughts in our head.

All these energy arcs become weaker as they curve out, though they may extend as much as twelve to fifteen feet from people who are feeling loved and loving and are in good health.

> *The power of electromagnetic energy*
> *A heart cell extracted from the heart and put in a solution to keep it living will keep a perfect rhythm with its heart, being within reach of that heart's electromagnetic field. Taken 'out of reach' of the heart vibration the single cell will begin to tremble and die.*
> **Dr Joseph Chilton Pearce**

When there is separation of mother and baby, even for an hour or two – and no one-to-one carer within reach – the electromagnetic support and protection is lost. This will often lead to a sense of confusion and abandonment. Feeling abandoned is the worst fear of all for a baby or young child. This fear must be understood and avoided at all costs, particularly in the vital first two months.

A baby in intensive care, without electromagnetic protection from the human heart, can be comforted by recorded non-stop womb sounds (see the resources list).

In a nutshell

All these new discoveries about the growth of the different parts of a baby's brain and the direct link between brain and heart are also about *us*. We carry our own babyhood within us, for better, for worse, for the rest of our lives. Understanding ourselves better will help us to understand our babies better. The more this chapter opens up our minds, the more we shall be able to give greater thought, as prospective parents, to our unborn babies and begin to communicate our understanding and therefore care for them from the time of conception.

There will also grow in us more understanding and loving human concern about the essential need to avoid any unwanted pregnancy, and also about the tragic and painful subject of abortion (see Appendix 5).

Highly recommended: *What Every Parent Needs to Know: the Incredible Effects of Love, Nurture and Play on Your Child's Development* by Margot Sunderland, 2016

www.margotsunderland.org

CHAPTER 7

Time in the Womb

THE AMAZING PACE AND ORDER OF YOUR BABY'S DEVELOPMENT

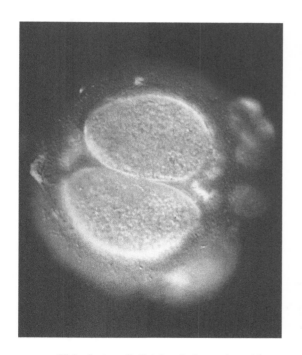 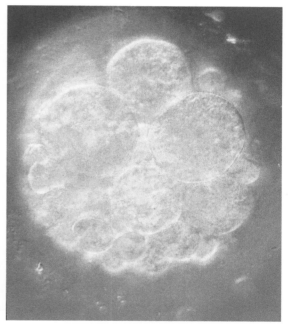

This first cell division takes place the moment the egg is fertilised on its way down
the fallopian tube to the womb

Almost at once, cells begin to clump together in groups to become different parts of a
minute body. A baby's brain is given a head start in development. By four weeks, the two
lobes of the brain are growing and there is the little dark line of a spine.

Then, very soon, there is the tiny pulse of the start of a heart... then a mouth that
opens and shuts.

Quickly, quickly, there's the shape of a liver, a pancreas, a stomach, intestines, buds of lungs and the parts of the brain that organise movement, smell, taste and remembering.

Every moment of the day there are leaps forward.

In the sixth week, there are minute twitches of movement.

By seven weeks, eyes and ears are growing and temporary kidneys are at work filtering and cleaning (these are replaced by bigger, better ones later).

The ovaries or testes develop. The baby is already a girl or a boy.

After two months, bones begin to form. Tiny hands and feet are stretching out in every direction. Muscles are building. Glands develop to organise and balance everything that is happening.

THERE IS A GYMNAST INSIDE!

From the third month the nerves in a baby's spinal cord have grown long enough to make contact with his muscles. The sense of touch comes quickly with all the touch receptors around his mouth and in his fingers.

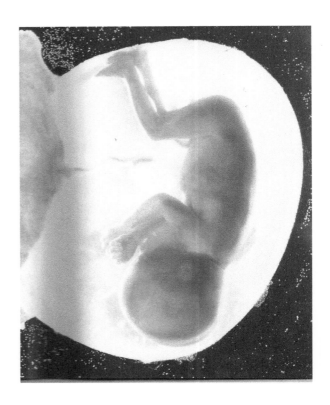

By the time your baby has been growing for seven months in the womb more than a hundred billion nerve cells will have formed ready to become brain cells and form 'branches' to receive and send signals to other brain cells and to muscles all over the body. They make contact and connect with each other using chemical messengers and electrical impulses. The speed of all this and your baby's growing consciousness is incredible.

Soon, your baby starts to have 'training sessions', bringing all his muscles into play in alternate bouts of exercising and resting. Many babies develop their own dance routine and practise for minutes at a time.

ALL THE SENSES COMING TO LIFE

Touch, taste and smell

Your baby is being touched and rubbed by the velvety and expanding walls holding him in place. His sense of being moulded into your body has increased day by day.

The whole of the baby's face and body is now sensitive except for his back and the top of his head. If your baby touches his own lips with an arm or a hand, he will begin to suck. He begins to taste the various 'seepage' food flavours in the amniotic fluid, according to what his mother has been eating. This is another reason why it is important to eat a variety of fresh, whole foods when we are pregnant. The baby is getting used to and beginning to enjoy the taste of them. This is practice for the real food he will be starting to eat within the next year.

By fourteen weeks there are 5,000 taste buds ready on the edge of the baby's tongue, on the roof of his mouth and in his upper throat. The baby is receiving forty calories of nourishment a day from sipping and swallowing up to forty millilitres of amniotic fluid per hour. This fluid is continually being renewed, with all its nutrients. Fresh bathwater and new tastes every day!

Between four and six months, the protective plugs protecting the baby's nostrils disappear and substances in the amniotic fluid can be smelt by the growing number of receptor cells in the baby's nose.

Hearing

A baby's ears start developing four weeks after conception. By four months he begins to respond to different sounds and may startle, blink, suddenly become still or have a slower heart rate for a moment. He can distinguish between different kinds of music and can recognise not only his mother's voice but also the voices of someone else who is close and familiar – his father, a grandparent or whoever is there talking to his mother on a regular basis. By six months, a baby can hear 65% of the sounds of a normal conversation taking place close to his mother.

Your unborn baby's ears are like a private telephone line, listening in to every sound in your body and voice! Your body sounds are like a familiar, well-loved

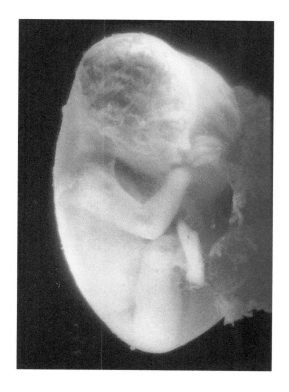

orchestra. The 'shushing' noises of a mother's blood circulation, digestive system and heartbeat together add up to seventy decibels – just about the same as switching on the vacuum cleaner. Your voice will have become familiar and have a real influence on your baby's feelings of security and peace. When your voice is soft and friendly, there will be a feeling of 'rightness'. Whenever your voice becomes shrill, angry or fearful, he will pick up your stress.

Humming, singing, speaking softly and playing gentle music – no loud rock – during your pregnancy will make a great difference to the ease with which he settles down after birth and how he develops right through childhood.

If you tell the same stories or rhymes to your unborn baby, or sing the same songs again and again, those stories and songs will hold his attention and calm him after he is born. If you change the words in the story or use the 'wrong' tune, your baby or toddler will know it and may react quite differently.

Music by, for example, Mozart and Vivaldi seems to quieten babies. Rock music and loud orchestral music may make a baby move and kick quite violently. Your familiar voice is the best music of all – even better than Mozart or Vivaldi.

The reason why we tend to disbelieve the ability of an unborn baby to hear so clearly from the womb is because, when we are adult, we have air in the tubes of our ears and therefore cannot hear well at all when we swim underwater. But an unborn baby still has water and no air in his ear tubes. As water is an excellent conductor of sound, he can hear accurately and clearly. In this respect, an unborn baby is more like a little dolphin in the sea than a human being. It is very special when parents sing or play a musical instrument to their unborn child.

When we are little, most of us are uninhibited - we jump around and sing and shout. But getting older can make us feel awkward about singing and humming songs and tunes we love. When we become pregnant and then have a baby in our arms we are given the best chance to get ourselves over any inhibitions we have and to start singing. Everyone in the world can sing if they are able to hear. Singing has a special effect on us and on our babies - even before birth. Singing comes from a different part of our brain than speaking. The vibrations of singing running through our bodies can do a power of good. They can change the way we feel and the way we think. They can steady us and give us confidence. They can make us feel happy and positive.

A sung-to baby will grow contented and easy. The familiarity of a tune and the words heard again and again can make any baby or young child, wherever they are in the world, feel soothed and blissful. If they are not well they feel comforted. Singing can also get you going, trying new things, which you may have wanted to do but never got round to.

A mother and music teacher

Seeing

A baby's eyes begin to link up with the brain and prepare for sight through tiny electrical impulses. However, these electrical impulses are vulnerable and the pattern of this fine connection can be disturbed by the mother smoking, drinking or taking drugs.

By six months, your baby's eyes are able to open and he can dimly see changes in light and shade when you are in bright sunshine and wearing thin clothing.

YOUR UNBORN BABY'S MEMORY, INTELLIGENCE AND UNDERSTANDING

'Memories' of sensations and new experiences of touch, taste, movement and sound – and also of any disturbance or shock to his sense of peace and safety – are beginning to build up months before he is born.

The brainstem of an unborn baby is so full of receptors that we know that 'memory' is there even in the first three months. It is the brainstem which will control the baby's breathing, heart rate and the nerves and muscles that are needed to see, to hear, to walk, to talk and to eat. The part of his brain which is his 'emotional centre' is fully grown by the fourth month.

By seven months, the brain is growing faster every day. Little flashes of personality begin to show. There may be an instant response, which you will be able to feel, to music, to familiar voices and to loud noises. Your baby is finger-sucking, repetitively practising chosen movements and favourite positions for rest. He is dreaming more. All these things encourage the electrical/chemical contacts between his billions of new brain cells.

Nerves are working like little telephone wires carrying messages of every kind to and from every cell in his body. In each one of those brain cells and body cells, these messages are stored and held.

Memories of our time in the womb and of our actual birth – whether we are able to recall them or not – are carried with us forever, not just in our brain cells but in every nerve and cell in our bodies.

Noticing what's going on

When you pay close attention to your growing baby you may discover how and when he shifts from one state to the next in your womb. There seem to be four easily recognised states:

1. Deep sleep when there's no movement from your baby and no response to anything going on 'outside'.
2. Little jerky, repeating movements, like hiccoughs, as if your baby is doing exercises in an organised way.

3. Big energetic movements as if your baby is climbing the wall of the uterus and testing all his joints.

4. A quiet, alert state when it feels as if your baby is 'listening' to you and 'feeling' what's going on. He may respond with movement to the sound of your voice and the feel of your hands touching and stroking the drum of your belly.

Towards the end of your pregnancy, when your womb is becoming much heavier, it is wise not to sleep on your back but to use a pillow at your back to keep you sleeping on your left side. Recent evidence shows that this position protects your baby through allowing your heart to work freely and assure the proper circulation of blood, oxygen and nutrients through the placenta. For more details, look at www.sciencedaily.com and www.nhs.uk/news/pregnancy-and-child/pregnant-women-should-avoid-sleeping-back-last-trimester/

A baby's movements inside the womb sometimes seem like a delicate dance if his mother is relaxed and unworried and is moving around calmly in her daily tasks. Tension and hurry in mothers, at home or out in the streets, can be reflected in twitches and startled movements building up in an unborn baby. The same sort of patterns will continue after your baby is born. The same sensations of uncertainty and loneliness can be passed down and continue even into the next generation unless recovery and healing can happen now.

This is the biggest reason why expectant mums should think seriously about how long they stay in work before the birth if that work is stressful and exhausting for them.

Your touch and your voice

During pregnancy your baby's brain is growing at a great pace. You can help his brain development during pregnancy by talking to and stroking your bulging tum and playing rhythmic and gentle music to him. Are there children around or close family members to share these things with you? Involving them is wonderful for everyone. Your baby will recognise their voices when he is born and feel truly welcomed into the world.

Not only can a baby feel his parents touching him through the walls of the womb, he can also sense the love in their hands and hear the warmth in their voices. Soon, he becomes able to sense their feelings for him

and for each other. A newborn baby already knows a lot about the relationship between his parents. He will soon know if they love each other or if and when there is conflict between them.

His sensations of feeling safe and happy will grow directly from the love between his parents and their love for him. If he is not being thought about, cared about, or looked forward to by his parents, those sensations will be of loneliness and uncertainty.

Prolonged and severe strain between a baby's parents can even reduce the mother's blood flow to the placenta and restrict her baby's growth.

When parents understand how their own stressful relationship can be passed to their unborn child and the lasting harm that this can cause, they might choose with real purpose to do all they can during pregnancy to lighten up the difficulties and to respect and help each other.

This will also have given their baby the inner confidence needed for the birth. A child who has been lovingly protected from feeling uncertain about life before birth will recover from the alarms and pressure of being born more quickly and easily.

The sensation of being welcomed before birth is very powerful.

Gentleness, patience, fairness, courage, trust and fun

These are the human qualities that will help him to grow up helpful, creative and kind. Your baby begins to learn these qualities from you before he is born.

A baby can't hear your thoughts, but when you speak them out, he gets the 'feel' of them clearly through the way you are speaking.

The more you talk out loud to your unborn child – especially about whatever loving thoughts and longings are in your heart, as well as about what you are doing at any moment and about cheerful plans, happy memories, mistakes you make and funny thoughts – the closer you will grow to each other and the more you will enjoy each other in the future. This is not foolish, it comes from thousands of years of instinct and experience.

After he is born, he will learn even more about these things by the way you talk to him, look at him, smile at him, handle him and steer him away calmly, again and again, from greed, selfishness, unkindness and any sign of cruelty and aggression as he grows older.

This is tough stuff!

An anxious and distressed pregnancy can lead to the birth of an often crying baby who may later, in childhood, show distress at every difficulty he meets and be hard to calm down. It may also lead him to hang back or retreat from new experiences and exploration, even simple things like being outside in wild weather.

If we can recognise this, we will then understand how important it is to do our very best and to keep trying to sort out our own troubles and tensions so that they are not transferred to our baby.

Search through the helplines and organisations that will be able to help you in the resource lists at the end of this book.

Occasionally a child is able to keep in their conscious memories – for the first few years – some clear memories of their own birth. Once they have words to use and are questioned, they may describe what happened first and what happened next and who did what.

Spontaneous memories can occasionally burst out of very young children, even when they can only talk a little.

> *Two mothers were once walking along the pavement together in the sunshine, talking about childbirth. They were holding hands with Alastair, the two-year-old son of one of them. Alastair's mother, wanting to include him in the conversation going on above his head, asked, 'Can you remember what was it like being born, Alistair?' 'Yes!' he said at once. 'My head hurt!'*

A baby in the womb does have a strong sense already about what it is like to be alive, to be growing and to feel loved and safe. Young children, all over the world, have drawn – uninvited, when their fingers become capable enough – extraordinary pictures of the different stages of their own growth in the womb. Many children know and remember what it felt like and some are able to draw these 'feeling memories' as pictures.

David Chamberlain, a neo-natal researcher in the United States – who sadly died in 2014 – said:

> *From all our studies, we know that babies are far more sophisticated than anything we ever gave them credit for being before. We didn't think they could have an experience and remember it.*
>
> *We didn't think they could sense anything and we didn't think they had brains enough and 'connections' enough to know and to hold onto what their senses were telling them.*
>
> *Now we do know it. We know that before they are born, babies have a working mind which is part of their human consciousness, their own SELF and SPIRIT. We now know they hold memories in every cell in their tiny bodies. We know that a newborn is recording everything that happens to him.*
> **www.birthpsychology.com (the Association for Prenatal and Perinatal Psychology and Health)**

Here is a story which shows also how much an unborn baby is hearing, absorbing, feeling and remembering while still in the womb – especially during the last three months before birth:

A while ago, I met a music teacher in London. She described how one of the best times of her life had been when her husband had been working in Jakarta in Indonesia. They were newly married and she was soon expecting their first child. They lived in a small hill village, a few miles from Jakarta. The women in the village taught her Indonesian songs while they gathered around the stone communal wash tank in the market square to scrub and rinse their clothes and linen. One song they taught her, a love song, was so beautiful that she sang it again and again all through her pregnancy. It somehow encapsulated the depth of her happiness at that time.

Then, two weeks before her baby was due to be born, everything changed without warning – her husband was recalled to London to work in a different department. She instinctively knew she must stop singing all the Indonesian songs she had learnt and leave behind any Indonesian possessions in order not to carry back the grief she felt at having to leave that place and those Indonesian friends. She knew she must turn all her attention to this very different life in London with their baby.

Three years later, on a summer morning, their little daughter was sitting quietly alone in the sandpit in the yard below their kitchen window. Suddenly, her mum in the kitchen heard a little hesitant voice starting to sing. At first just a few Indonesian words then the whole of the Indonesian love song that had been her 'theme song' throughout her pregnancy. She knew her child had heard her singing it again and again every day in the womb but never, ever, since then.

Sarah Woodhouse

CHAPTER 8

Making Choices for your Baby's Birth

HOW CAN I HAVE THE BEST POSSIBLE BIRTH?

All mothers hope for the least stressful birth for their own sake and for their baby's. It is natural to want a straightforward, easy as possible beginning to your baby's life. However, the strange thing is that babies are designed to withstand powerful squeezing and pressure during the birth process and that this even helps them to prepare for being born. The pressure starts off the big changes in their body which will be necessary for living outside the womb. These include the way that blood circulates round their body and breathing air for the first time. It is also thought that the whole process of birth switches on other reflexes, like sucking and crying, which are needed for survival. Babies who are born by caesarean section do not experience this pressure and may need a great deal of sensitive handling and holding to help introduce them to life outside the womb.

The best birth of all is a normal or 'natural' birth.

Natural birth

Natural birth is birth which starts spontaneously, continues throughout labour and delivery, without risk and without medical intervention. A normal birth is when a baby is born head down (vertex position), without interference, after thirty-seven to forty-two weeks of pregnancy. The benefits of a natural birth are less discomfort, a quick recovery and a great sense of achievement for you, and a baby who soon starts to suckle, to gaze intently at your face and to settle peacefully into your arms.

A natural birth can also make a great difference to your whole family.

I was knocked over by the depth of bottomless love that took over the moment I held Lizzie in my arms for the first time. Nothing had ever crashed into my heart in such a way. I'd never felt anything like that in my life.
Patrick, a first-time dad

What can make this more likely?

One person present throughout a woman's labour who is peacefully there, sitting calmly and quietly, perhaps doing something rhythmic, like knitting or sewing, will have a very valuable effect on the mother. This person's presence and her calm will help to keep the mother's level of adrenaline (the stress hormone) as low as possible and increase her levels of oxytocin (the love hormone) necessary for an easy birth.

This could be your midwife, your doula, your mother, your sister or a close and trusted friend.

Rethinking the way we support mothers during labour

Many obstetricians believe that a caesarean birth can be better for mother and baby than the possibility of interference in other ways during labour – such as induction, drugs, examinations and the use of forceps.

For positive changes in childbirth, as a society we need to rethink how we can best help mothers during labour, birth and the first hours. We need to understand the processes of birth more fully and clearly and how to support the emotional, the instinctive and the animal needs that are in every one of us.

When a baby is born it faces swarms of bacteria it has never met before. A caesarean birth prevents your baby from absorbing vital gut flora (bacteria) from his mother during the second stages of labour. This gut flora plays a big part in protecting your baby from allergies and infections, especially during his first year. It helps to set up his healthy digestive system and immune system for the future. This link will tell you how this works and what can be done to protect your caesarean birth baby:

www.newscientist.com/article/2075768-boost-c-section-babies-by-giving-them-vaginal-bacteria/

The feeling of oneness

A natural birth encourages full and immediate production of helpful hormones called oxytocin (calming) and endorphins (pain relieving). These give support to mother and baby during the birth and after the birth. They help build a mother's confidence about mothering and breastfeeding and her instant and deep bonding with her baby.

A long, hard birth or complications needing medical help – and the extra exhaustion that is likely to follow – can delay this instant and deep bonding for a little while.

In the womb, your baby has felt utterly, completely and wholly part of you. After he is born he can feel the anxiety of separation for the first time.

But, when you hold your baby against you, heart-to-heart, your love connects; when you hold your baby cheek-to-cheek, your spirits touch; when you hold your baby skin-to-skin whenever possible, your energy is shared. The feeling of oneness comes back. Your baby will feel calm and balanced.

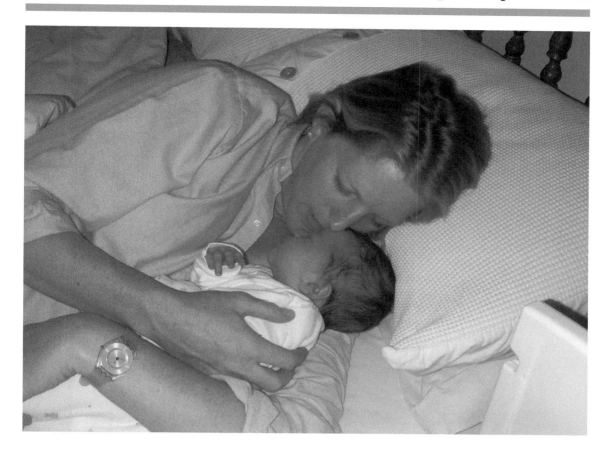

This closeness and loving touch will also help you both to recover from any birth trauma either of you have suffered.

A natural anxiety about the birth

Most women fear giving birth because they believe that the pain may prove to be more than they can manage. They may have heard horror stories and feel more anxious than confident about their own natural ability to give birth.

It is natural to feel anxious. If it is your first baby you will never have experienced anything like it before. Even if this is not your first baby, experience may not have given you the chance, opportunity and support you needed to give birth using your own inner strength and resources.

It is reassuring to know that when women are in a relaxing environment, with privacy and continuous loving support, the majority of women can give birth without any help at all.

Watching a birth on television can give a distorting perspective because it can feel intrusive and may have been over-dramatised to spice up the storyline. Those who have had the chance to watch the natural and magical moment of an animal's birth – a cow with her calf, a horse with her foal, a sheep with her lamb, or puppies and kittens being born – will have witnessed the birthing instincts of the mother animal working perfectly and the instant bonding and care which follows. Watching animals give birth can be especially wonderful for children because they are still not so far from their own birth.

WHO WILL BE THERE TO SUPPORT YOU BEFORE, DURING AND AFTER THE BIRTH?

You may know when you become pregnant who is closest to you and who might be glad and able to be in regular touch with you, and then be a calm presence at the birth of your baby and afterwards. Whoever this person is, they will be there to give you comfort, encouragement and practical help. It might be your own mother, your husband, your partner, a happy and steady friend or neighbour who has given birth herself and has good memories, or an experienced doula.

If you can't think of anyone to be your doula, perhaps there might be someone you get to know through Netmums, a nearby children's centre or the clinic you are attending. You need to find someone who you feel is right to ask to be your birth partner.

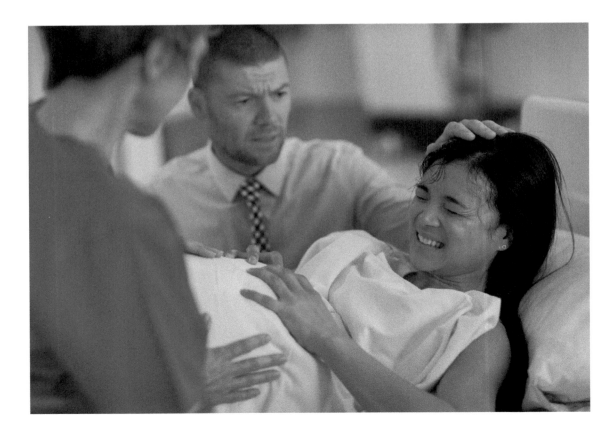

What is a doula?

The word 'doula' is a Greek word meaning 'a woman who is a caregiver' – someone who mothers the mother. Doulas are trained and experienced in childbirth and are there to provide practical and emotional support to you and the father of your child in your home or in hospital, before, during and after the birth.

The midwife and medical staff are responsible for the clinical aspects of your pregnancy and birth. Your doula will be there to be a calm and comforting presence. She will steady you, hold you, rub your back, listen to you and fetch what you need. She will also be there to listen to and to teach the father how he can best give his confident and loving support during the different stages of birth. After the birth, your doula will help in all sorts of practical ways, perhaps holding your baby while you have a shower, making tea for you both and protecting your privacy. She will also help you both to recognise the clues your new baby is giving you to show you what he needs. A doula, or whoever you have to mother you, will help you to feel part of something big, precious and good.

The doula movement has been steadily growing since 1998, and represents the recovery of an age-old way of caring for women during pregnancy, childbirth and early motherhood.

I was feeling really weepy and exhausted a week after the birth, when my doula walked in. She looked at my face, put her arms round me and began to talk to me. 'Look what you've done,' she said. 'Look what you are doing... you are a marvel!' I just felt completely different.
A mother with her first baby

It's the best job satisfaction you could ever hope for! I believe postnatal doula care should be made available free to everyone after birth because of the fantastic effect of this care and friendship. The mother's confidence grows, there is better bonding between mother and baby, there is much less likelihood of postnatal depression. There is easier and longer breastfeeding and therefore a healthier, happier baby.
A doula in London

The big secret is to help a mother stay calm.
A doula in Leeds

Birth can be anything from a horror story, to the most beautiful, profound, loving experience imaginable. I became a doula because I wanted to make a difference to the lives of women, babies and fathers, knowing that this crucial time has such impact on a family's future. My training as a doula was a time of deep growth.

I feel if families, globally, had the support they truly needed, everyone felt safe at the birth, and if bonding was undisturbed, this would radically change the way we live and look after each other.

Listening and watching for what is needed and helping a woman at birth, I get to learn about love. It's wonderful to be closely involved from the pregnancy to the final postnatal visits where the parents are confident and have outgrown their need for a doula.

I loved the holistic approach. The first few families to trust me as their doula gave me the best gift ever.

Phobe Gladstone

Many mothers who have had a doula to steady and comfort them have been inspired to become doulas themselves.

Potentially every woman, whether trained or not, can support another woman. How well she does this depends on the warmth of her heart and the depth of her pregnancy-and-birth wisdom and knowledge as well as the training she receives to become a registered doula. It is her quiet presence that will make the mother feel safe.

Being a doula may be easier for those who have themselves experienced giving birth, breastfeeding and rearing children. However, there are some women who do not have this experience of motherhood who become wonderfully nurturing doulas. A pregnant woman should be able to choose the doula with whom she is most comfortable – even if this is a close and loving member of her family or a neighbour.

When there is a high birth rate and a shortage of midwives, there is an increase in stress and insecurity for mothers. The use of epidural pain-killing injections and caesarean sections is often a direct result of a mother's anxiety due to the lack of one-to-one emotional support for her during the birth.

Oxytocin – the hormone that helps a mother to give birth – is the same hormone that helps her to enjoy sex. Just as anxiety and stress can put a woman off sex, it can also put her off or slow down her labour.

In Hull, the Goodwin Volunteer Doula Project has been responding to this understanding and has trained volunteer doulas who work without pay for single mothers from poorer communities. This has been so successful it is also being launched in other places.

Sherrie spent nine months in the grip of postnatal depression when the youngest of her three children was just six months old.

> *There were times when I thought if I was dead, it would be so much easier for everyone. My children didn't have a mum, not really, for nine months. My husband had to run the house and go to work because I just couldn't do anything.*

After Sherrie was given round-the-clock support and when she had recovered, she attended an outreach doula course. Three years later, she became a volunteer doula.

> *Someone from the hospital said that having another woman present at the birth to give support can help with postnatal depression and that clicked with me. If I can help prevent another woman going through what happened to me, then I'll do it.*

See Appendix 4: 'Baby Blues' and Postnatal Depression.
   To find a doula and to learn more, see:

* www.doula.org.uk
  Doula UK is an independent, voluntary network of doulas, providing a communication link for all those who are doulas or who would like to become doulas. The project provides a doula map
* www.nurturingbirthdirectory.com
  Find a Doula provides a doula consultancy service and offers training by people with a nursing/teaching background.
* www.dona.org
  Dona International provides the same information and services primarily in the USA. You may find other resources locally.

Plan for the best, but be prepared for anything!

If you have been in tune with your baby throughout pregnancy you may already be developing feelings about what sort of birth is right for you both.

   Tell the midwife and everyone present what you feel and what your wishes are and then, if unforeseen problems do arise, the medical support you will be offered is more likely to be understanding and in line with your hopes and feelings.

Medical intervention

Of course, sometimes medical interventions are needed. What matters then is that you feel involved in the decisions being made and can understand the reasons why particular medical interventions are proposed. There is no reason ever to feel a failure if this must happen.

> *I had an undetected growth in my cervix which narrowed the birth canal too much for my baby's head to come through. I had to have a last-minute caesarean. It saved his life. All I felt was massive relief and thankfulness.*

Avoiding the use of drugs whenever possible

With loving one-to-one help and encouragement in preparing for the birth during your pregnancy, there will be less need for drugs during labour. The ongoing support of your midwife and of a doula or wise close friend (maybe a mum herself) will make all the difference to the birth and your recovery afterwards.

There are all kinds of skills and practices which can prepare you for a birth with less pain and anxiety and therefore less need for medical intervention. These might be hypnotherapy, pilates and yoga for expectant mums (Birthlight), homeopathy and herbal support and massage.

If you would prefer to give birth without medical pain relief, there are many good alternatives.

THERE ARE LOTS OF THINGS THAT WORK BETTER THAN DRUGS!

Here are some examples:

- ♥ Feeling loved, safe and supported throughout your pregnancy.
- ♥ Birth hypnotherapy: www.natalhypnotherapy.co.uk
- ♥ Massaging the perineum (pelvic floor) with olive oil during the weeks before birth.
- ♥ Peace and privacy to allow your birthing instincts to take over from your busy mind.
- ♥ As little talking as possible and try to avoid timing and counting contractions. Both these activities can pull you back from feeling the changing rhythms of birth and going with it.
- ♥ TENS (Transcutaneous Electrical Nerve Stimulation) machine – with pads which fix to your back (see the resources list).
- ♥ Acupuncture and Acupressure (see the resources list).
- ♥ Being able to walk, move around and try all the positions, especially upright positions with gravity to help you, will ease the discomfort. Follow your instincts, moment by moment.
- ♥ Being massaged and stroked where and when you ask for it.

♥ Loving and passionate kisses during labour. When you kiss the man you love, you loosen up and relax at the top and you loosen up down below, too!
♥ Listening to peaceful music that you know and love and which can help to relax you.

Any drugs given to you during labour will also affect your baby. Some can cause respiratory problems, feeding difficulties and failure of your baby to bond easily and quickly with you – also with his dad. Perhaps, saddest of all, is that the amazing joy of those first moments of welcome and intimacy immediately after birth may be lost.

Some medical interventions can also make others more likely to follow. For example, an induced birth can make it more likely that you will need an epidural (anaesthetic injection in your back). Having an epidural can make it more likely that your baby will need forceps or ventouse (a vacuum cup placed on the baby's head) for the final stages of birth. This chain reaction is probably because the natural birthing rhythm of your body has been interfered with.

You can ask not to have your baby induced unless there is an urgent medical reason to do so.

If medical intervention turns out to be essential, your baby will cope better if you – or someone caring for you both – is talking to him gently. It's important to remember that babies can hear voices from the womb and during their birth surprisingly clearly, especially the tone of the voice and especially if that voice is speaking love and encouragement.

Particularly babies born to mothers who have been given drugs while they are pregnant or during labour will need almost continuous skin-to-skin contact, stroking, touching and suckling to ease them into life. They may need this for a week or two, or even longer. They may sleep and sleep at first with the effects of the drugs and later become fretful and distressed. It may take time, but continuous touch and closeness, hearing Mum and Dad's familiar voices and seeing their smiling faces will do a lot to heal any harm that has been done.

FINDING OUT ABOUT YOUR OWN BIRTH

Everything that ever happened to us in our lives influences us. The way we ourselves were conceived, born and welcomed into the world will surge up again in us. Long and deeply buried memories of our own birth journey and the huge experience of being born – the pressure, the discomfort, possibly the fear and pain for some of us – will come surging up again, whether consciously or unconsciously, once we are expecting a baby ourselves.

This is why it is important for expectant mums and dads to talk to their own parents if possible and find out about their own birth. Who was there at your birth to help your mother, to hold you, care for you, welcome you?

When expectant parents are able to talk to their own mother and hear a little about their own birth it might help them to know more clearly what choices they want to make for themselves for the sake of their own baby when he is being born.

Surprisingly, birth often happens in ways which are related to what happened at the birth of the father, rather than at the birth of the mother. This is simply because the father's support and inner peace and hopefulness have such a profound effect on the mother's ability to relax and to give birth easily and with confidence.

Some fathers may have had such a rough birth experience themselves, that being present for their own baby's birth may seem too overwhelming to face. They will usually know instinctively that they would not be able to give the emotional support needed and want to keep well away when contractions begin in earnest.

However, with the loving support of a known and trusted midwife or doula, a severely birth-anxious father can be given the opportunity to discover how much his own birth had continued to affect him. With the experience of joy and amazement at the beautiful birth of his own child he can be healed and find new courage and confidence.

Where would you like the birth to be?

Choosing the right place to have your baby is a very personal decision. If a choice is possible, talk to your midwife, investigate each possibility and think about it carefully.

Try to visit different places where you could give birth. You may have a choice of local hospitals. There may also be a birth centre near you. Some hospitals have special units run by midwives for women who are hoping for a natural birth. These are sometimes called 'low-risk' units.

If your pregnancy has been straightforward and there is not a dire shortage of midwives where you live, you can ask for a home birth, especially if you have a doula or member of your family to support you.

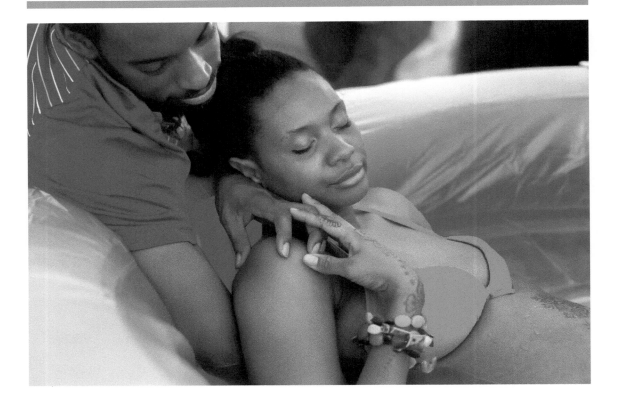

Home births

One of the best things about home births is that everyone in the family is around. Older children, if there are any, can learn so much about birth and be involved and part of the excitement, the welcome and the tender care of the newborn baby.

There are lots of advantages to having a home birth.

- You can labour and give birth in familiar surroundings. You are likely to be more relaxed and this can help your labour to move on steadily from one stage to the next.
- When contractions start, you don't have to decide when to go to hospital or face a journey. You won't have to pack anything.
- You will probably be looked after in turn by midwives who will have got to know you during your pregnancy. They will also look after you in the days following the birth of your baby.
- You may find labour less painful and will therefore be less likely to want pain-relieving drugs.
- You will be less likely to need medical interventions.
- Your husband or partner will be more likely to be around to give you support and will be there at night, instead of miles away maybe.

- If you have older children, you will not need to leave them or worry about a toddler missing you and becoming distressed. When a new baby does not separate a mother from her other child or children, there is usually less jealousy and it is easier to give needed attention and reassurance.

Home births – where they always used to be – have recently become more popular all over the world. But hospital births will always be safest if you have had a difficult pregnancy and there are still possible complications.

My home birth

Before I became pregnant, I was very scared of childbirth, expecting it to be long and painful. I also thought that people who chose to have their baby at home, especially the first one, were crazy and irresponsible. I thought that women who chose to give birth without an epidural were masochists. Why endure pain for nothing?

Then, when I was five months pregnant, two things happened to me. I attended a Birthlight childbirth preparation course and I met and hired my birth doula, Maddie. I wanted to have a doula because I thought that being looked after in a hospital by midwives who you had not even met before would not make you feel relaxed and that would be stressful. Maddie lent me Ina May Gaskin's book called Ina May's Guide to Childbirth. This book was so great. It gave me a different perspective – that it was not all just discomfort and pain. Michel Odent's book Birth Reborn: What Childbirth Should Be helped me to make my own decisions about the birth I wanted. I decided to be at home for the birth.

I was also lucky to have had a supportive and understanding midwife who came to feel like a real friend.

I finally lost my fear of the birth during the last few weeks of my pregnancy, helped by the Birthlight antenatal yoga, discussions and using a device called the Epi-No Delphine to prepare for childbirth and take away the fear of tearing. Perhaps it was also the birth hormones building up in my body! I applied for a home birth.

I gave birth 16 days later than expected. My midwife knew I did not want to be induced, and respected that. I was excited and not at all fearful when the contractions began! Again, I am so grateful for Maddie's and the midwife's support during that time.

My labour was 30 hours long and it was hard work and it was painful. But I never felt scared. Maddie's support was wonderful. She made me feel cared for and safe. She also helped Chi to support me. I felt I could cope, even when the pain was strong. I used a TENS machine and moaned to help me through the contractions. Maddie and Chi took turns to hold a warm rice bag on my tummy. I also found I spent much of my labour standing up holding onto the banisters. I was always encouraged to follow my instincts and to do what felt right for me at the time.

When my son was born, he was able to come gently into the world. The lights were dimmed and the voices hushed. He was left to lie undisturbed on my tummy for an hour after birth. His cord was left intact to finish pulsing before being cut. It was the most amazing experience of my life.

The few days after the birth were so special and peaceful at home with just me, Chi and our new baby son.

Sophie Messager

For information about how to purchase or hire the TenS machine:
www.babycentre.co.uk/a542581/using-a-tens-machine-in-labour

For information about the Epi-No Delphine device:
www.epi-no.co.uk

Birth centres

Birth centres are small maternity units approved by the Baby Centre Medical Advisory Board. They are staffed and, in most cases, run by midwives who believe that most women can give birth without medical help. They provide a relaxed and safe environment for giving birth in an atmosphere that is friendly, informal and unhurried. The excellent postnatal care in birth centres also means that you are more likely to get breastfeeding off to a good start and to breastfeed your baby for longer.

> *Midwives who work in birth centres, and who run these centres themselves, have a completely different birth philosophy to midwives who are stuck with a shift system, in large teams that are part of a rigid hospital hierarchy. They know how to keep birth normal. That is the most important thing.*
> **Sheila Kitzinger, author of** Birth Your Way

The good news is that some hospitals are now opening midwife-led birth centres alongside their conventional or 'consultant-led' maternity units.

To find out about birth centres near where you live, search www.babycentre.co.uk.

Hospital birth

Regrettably, in many hospitals – except in a Unicef Baby Friendly Hospital – it is less easy to have a natural birth. If you would like to try for as natural a birth as possible in hospital, make sure you have your own birth plan written down and show it to whoever is looking after your pregnancy and birth. This list will include specific requests, such as being able to move around freely during labour and allowing your baby to remain with you, skin-to-skin after the birth.

These DVDs can help you, in different ways, to make choices for your pregnancy and the birth of your baby.

- *Gentle Birth Choices*, with Barbara Harper, RN
- *Understanding Childbirth*, with Betty Parsons, MBE
- *The Essential Babycare Guide*, Professor Robert Winston

The next chapter is all about deciding where your baby will sleep for the next few months.

~ CHAPTER 9 ~

Where will my baby sleep?

The absolutely best place for your new baby to be during the day is in your arms, in a sling or else close beside you so that whenever he wakes up he can see your smile, hear your voice and smell you when you bend over him.
Maude, a grandma

LET'S SPEND THE NIGHT TOGETHER

'Bed sharing' is sometimes called 'sleep sharing'. The instinct and need to sleep together has been with us forever and continues, the same as ever, in many cultures. It is the best of all choices for mums and babies.

The stress of separation for a newborn baby can be very severe and even a few yards of separation from Mum in those first weeks can seem like a football pitch away for a baby only recently out of the warm, safe closeness of the womb, and separated from all the internal sounds he had been hearing. Feeling your touch, hearing your breathing and your voice close by, and being able to smell you and see your smile, gives him the continuous and gentle reassurance he needs in the first few months of his life.

Babies cry significantly less while sleeping with or right beside their mothers compared with babies who are separated at night.

Because of the publicity and the concern about 'cot death' (Sudden Infant Death Syndrome) it is often forgotten that this almost always occurs when a baby is sleeping out of touch and alone or because of an undiscovered birth defect.

A baby's breathing and heart rate, by 2 months old, are more regular when sleeping next to mum than when sleeping alone with fewer dips in blood oxygen.
Dr Sears, Sleep Sharing Research 1993

If your husband or partner is anxious about the idea of bed sharing, you will need time to talk unhurriedly and plan this together; also talk with your midwife before you decide. Allow yourselves time to change your mind before the birth.

Some mothers who were themselves short of cuddles, kisses and closeness when they were babies may feel uneasy at the thought of bed sharing with their baby. If this is so for you, it is worth knowing that many mums have found that bed sharing with their own baby helps to heal them from the ancient sense of aloneness they are still feeling.

In the same way, sleeping together at night can comfort you both after a long, difficult, or caesarean birth, or if there was a medical problem, which meant you were separated from your baby for a few minutes or a few hours after the birth.

Increasing numbers of midwives, maternity nurses and mothers are now feeling relief that the alarmist attitude towards sharing a bed with your baby is beginning to change. The ancient and instinctive habit of looking after our newborn babies by sleeping with them at night and feeding them in darkness with minimal disturbance during the night is recognised as being natural and normal. *But you do need a big enough bed and have all the safety precautions in place.*

CHECKING OUT THE PHYSICAL RISKS OF BED SHARING

These are the physical things to think about before you decide to sleep with your baby in bed with you:

*A newborn baby should not bed share during the first few weeks –
perhaps up to eleven weeks:*

♥   *if he has been born early*
♥   *if he is underweight*
♥   *if his mum is overweight*
♥   *if the mattress is soft or saggy.*

*In which case, co-sleeping with an attached bedside crib is essential and is the best
way to 'sleep together'*

Sleeping together, the first night at home. Sturdy, full-term baby, 8 lbs.

♥ Could he get caught in the gap between your bed and the wall or wriggle his way to the open side of the bed and fall onto the floor? Suggestions: Check every night for gaps and never use a pillow to plug a gap or to stop him falling out of bed. If necessary, fold up your bed frame and put your mattress on the floor for a few months with perhaps a folded blanket alongside if your mattress is too small for three of you.

♥ Was he born prematurely or born small or frail? Suggestions: Only when he is bigger, sturdier and able to move his head is it safe to have him in bed with you.

♥ Are you sleeping on a soft, saggy mattress or a waterbed? There is a real danger here of a small baby being squashed or suffocated. The same danger exists if you fall deeply asleep on a sagging sofa or in an armchair, perhaps surrounded by cushions.

♥ Are you seriously overweight and your body therefore distorting the shape of your mattress? There is a real danger here that your baby could slip beneath you as you turn over in your sleep.

♥ There is a danger of overheating. A newborn baby is not able to sweat to cool himself if he gets too hot and, in bed beside you, he will be picking up your body heat. If you are sleeping under a warm duvet, he could become much too hot. You might not notice this happening to him in the middle of the night if you are sound asleep and at a comfortable temperature yourself. Suggestions: Note the temperature of your bedroom. Feel your baby's temperature with two fingers at his neck or on his tummy when you feed him or touch him during the night. This will tell you if he is becoming flushed and sweaty. If so, could he wear just a light vest and nappy, or be in his own sleeping bag with no other cover over him at all? You will soon learn what is right for him, depending also on whether it is winter or summer.

CHECKING OUT THE LIFESTYLE RISKS OF BED SHARING

There are serious risks to sleeping in the same bed with your baby...

If either parent is smoking at any time and anywhere. The 'secondary smoke' your baby will inhale from your breath and skin and clothes is now known to be harmful to tiny new lungs just when your baby is breathing for the first time and finding the rhythm of it.

If you or your husband or partner have been drinking alcohol and are therefore less sensitive to your baby because you will be sleeping too heavily.

❤ If you are unwell and on medication, or if you take recreational drugs, these will both make you drowsy and less responsive to your baby.

❤ If you are tired to the point of exhaustion, you could sleep so deeply that you lose your instinctive sense of where your baby is lying.

Any of the last three will dull your sensitivity to your baby. You could roll onto him as you sleep without growing instantly alert to his little uncomfortable wriggles and therefore realise that you are squashing him.

If you can eliminate all these risks and decide to have your baby in bed with you, you will be giving him all kinds of support:

❤ The stimulation of sleeping next to you will steady his breathing throughout the night.

❤ His sleep-wake patterns will begin to settle down to match yours as you feed him and sleep again during the night. Sleep with your baby's head level with your face or breast, ready for the next feed!

❤ His heart rate will steady and slow down as it needs to during the months following the birth.

❤ His metabolic rate, his digestive and circulation system and hormone levels, will settle down and find the right balance.

❤ His enzyme production, to help him build the antibodies he needs to fight infection, will develop as it should.

❤ Oxytocin and opioid (the anti-stress chemicals in your baby's brain) will be released, making him quicker and easier to calm whenever he shows little signs of stress.

When my baby was three months old I went back to work part time in the evenings. I would come home late and hear her doing a sort of panicky breathing with sudden gasps every 7 or 8 seconds. As soon as I picked her up and lay down in bed with her, she started breathing more calmly and regularly again. After a few more days I quit work and slept with her every night.
Emily

When you sleep with your baby you will find you only need to half-wake for about fifteen seconds to start feeding and then resettle yourself and your baby. This very brief period of semi-wakefulness, because it does not bring your brain to full alert, means that you will drop back to sleep again easily within a moment or two.

Sleep sharing matters more than ever if you are separated from your baby for several hours during the day. Sleeping together allows you to reconnect and make up for the missed 'touch time'. Also, the hormones that are produced in your body by your baby's sucking at night will help you relax and wind down after any hurrying and tension in your day.

It has been shown that most mothers and babies who sleep together tend to sleep curled up facing each other for most of the night and a baby is quick to squeak and struggle if his face is pressed against anything that stops him breathing even for a few seconds.

Compared with your baby's lifespan, the time he spends in your arms, at your breast and in your bed is very short. But the indelible memories of your love and availability will last a lifetime.

> *A baby is too little to sleep alone. Sleeping together makes babies happy. The parents' breathing affects the baby so sleeping together is good. It also helps you tell if your baby is too hot or too cold. You can hear your baby's sounds. You feel his movements when he wants to suck.*
> **A Chinese mother**

Research findings about bed sharing

Boys who slept with their parents as babies and toddlers grow up with significantly higher self-esteem and less anxiety. Girls who slept with their parents as babies and toddlers are more relaxed and easy and show more physical affection as adults.

Solitary sleeping children become harder to handle, deal less well with stress and grow more, not less, dependent on their parents. Children who have never been allowed to bed share are more anxious than children who have slept in their parents' bed when they were babies.

> *I have been told that many babies in America are made to sleep by themselves. This shocks me very much and fills me with pity, for this is child neglect.*
> **A Mayan woman**

CO-SLEEPING BEDSIDE CRIBS, THE BEST ALTERNATIVE

'Co-sleeping', on the other hand, means having your baby sleeping close-up beside you, within arms' reach, in a special bedside crib which levels with, and is securely attached to, your bed. Your baby is in his own safe space. You are still within smile, touch and breath reach of each other. Your baby can also smell you, which will make him feel secure, awake or asleep. Bed sharing or sleeping right beside each other like this will help your baby *thrive*. It will help him grow happier and kinder because his brain, his emotions, his personality and the inner spirit in him will be growing in the best possible ways.

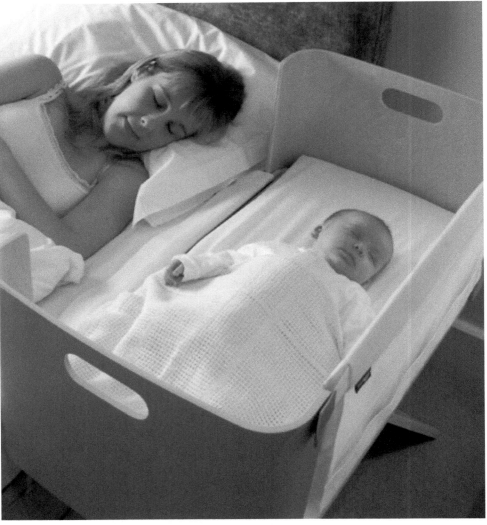

Imagine this in the darkness of the night

This physical closeness between you, day and night, is critically important during the first six months. After that time, the 'self-start' breathing mechanism in his brain will be doing fine. Until then, he could need you to be a warm, breathing 'pacemaker' close beside him.

> *The greatest blessing is the pleasure of sleeping with your baby and letting it nurse – how can you expect to hold onto your children later in life if you begin their lives by pushing them away? Sleeping with my baby lets me make up some time I couldn't spend with her during the day. It gives me more time to feed and nurture my baby.*
> **Eastern Kentucky mother**
>
> *The first few months between a mother and baby are the special ones – when every breath and smile helps cement a life-long bond.*
> **Richard Batson,** Eastern Daily Press

Out of reach at night

All young babies – even secure, much loved babies – feel frightened when they first wake up and there is no mum right there beside them. Unless mum is able instantly to touch and comfort, separation anxiety grows and grows, from a whimper to a wail of grief. If your baby is sleeping the far side of the room, or even in another room, this will jerk you awake with a thumping heart. Both of you are now probably wide awake and upset. It will be a struggle to give the comfort needed each time this happens, and exhaustion will grow in you. It takes much longer to settle a distressed baby than an instantly touched baby within arm's reach where you can breastfeed your baby back to deep sleep much more quickly and easily.

> *'I can usually start breastfeeding him just as he starts to squirm and reach for the nipple. Getting him to suck immediately keeps him from fully waking up, and then we both drift back to sleep right after feeding.'*
>
> *'I know we are on the same brainwave when we sleep together. We seem to be in perfect night-time harmony – and my life is so much easier than with my first baby.'*
>
> *'Our baby started to show symptoms of apnoea [the term used when a baby's breathing suddenly stops or becomes periodic because the stimulus from her brain to take another breath is still unreliable]. Breastfeeding, holding her a lot during the day and sleeping face-to-face together at night put an end to this worry.'*

'We discovered that we can help our baby's asthma by holding him in a "bear hug cuddle" and breathing slow and deep. This has become a valuable part of our asthma plan.'

The best start to life of all for a baby is to bed share with Mum – when everything is right for this – but also to have an attached Bednest crib to give your baby his own safe space. This can be for those times when you should not or do not want to bed share, for whatever good reason.

INTRODUCING THE BENEFITS OF THE BEDNEST

The Bednest was the first attached and levelling crib designed and marketed. Long and wide-ranging research into the most vital physical, emotional and spiritual needs of newborn babies and their mothers was undertaken by *Right from the Start*, a charity working in every possible way to 'help parents shine'. www.right-from-the-start.org

The Bednest is a small, sturdy bedside crib specially designed to keep mothers and their new babies at the same level and close enough to be within 'touch, breath, smell and heartbeat reach' throughout the night and when resting together during the day – yet allowing the baby his own safe space. This essential closeness follows naturally from the nine months in the womb and avoids the loneliness and stress of separation.

The Bednest won the Concept 2005 Design Award at the Baby & Child International Fair and was voted 'Best Buy' in *Mother & Baby* magazine, December 2008. In 2014 it was awarded the 2014 'Consumer Choice Bedside Cot' by Mumii. It can be hired for six months if you prefer not to buy one of your own.

www.bednest.eu for new and refurbished Bednests and all accessories.

'I think the Bednest is a wonderful idea. It gave me a lovely feeling to be so close to Fern and to be able to watch over her and touch her whenever I wanted. I'll never forget those first few nights as we settled down together, side-by-side.'

'I felt so safe and relaxed about everything. I could feed her whenever she showed she needed it, almost without moving in my bed. Lying there smiling at her every morning is perfect!'

'It was really hard settling down at night after all the excitement of the birth. It was as if I couldn't stop listening to his little snufflings all night long. I couldn't sleep so I put his crib in the sitting room so I couldn't hear him unless he started crying. It didn't feel right somehow and I had scary dreams.'

All co-sleeper cribs attach securely to your bed, level with your mattress. With a fold-down side they become a small extension to your own bed. The Bednest can be set at a slight tilt if your baby suffers from reflux or develops a stuffy cold. It also packs flat for easy travelling and storage.

A co-sleeping crib gives you the extra security of having a safe space ready to use, if and when you need it. If your baby is premature or low-weight, you can use a co-sleeper crib until he is sturdier and can safely sleep in bed with you at any time, perhaps after a dawn feed.

If you do find sleeping close together is disturbing you at first because you are being kept awake by your newborn's little snuffling noises, know that, in a few days, you will sleep right through these tiny sounds until your baby wakes and makes hunger noises. Sleeping close will become as natural as breathing. Would you feel able to persevere until you both settle down together and sleep peacefully?

My baby was 5 weeks premature. She was so tiny when she came home – and I'm quite fat – that sleeping with her was too risky. The Bednest was perfect. I used to go to sleep touching her as if my arm was a new umbilical cord for her. She thrived and put on weight steadily.
A mum with a five-month-old baby

Some babies become exceptionally lively when they are two to three months old. If your baby discovers how to wriggle-and-roll his way out of the Bednest to get closer to you again in the middle of the night (just when you have thankfully fallen asleep again after a feed!) make this simple barricade. Roll a towel tightly into a long 'sausage' and secure it with several strong elastic bands. Lay it along the line of the Bednest (or any other co-sleeper crib) where it touches your mattress – just as you might lay a draft excluder along the bottom of a door. You will still be able to comfort your baby with a touch of your hand.

See Resource List for other, recommended co-sleeper cribs.

THE MANY, SPECIAL BENEFITS OF SLEEPING CLOSE

♥ It encourages and helps you to breastfeed quietly and peacefully during the night. There will be minimal disturbance of any kind for the rest of the family and greater likelihood of a rapid return to sleep after feeds for you both. This will give you many more hours of undisturbed sleep each week.

♥ Babies who sleep close beside their mothers breastfeed more successfully and for longer. This will be of great benefit to the health of you both.

♥ Babies have the pleasure of hearing familiar voices close by and being frequently touched and stroked, whether asleep or awake. This touching and stroking is a crucial element in their settling, contentment and the healthy development of their brain and personality.

♥ When a baby is able to breathe in minute quantities of the carbon dioxide breathed out by a parent holding them or sleeping beside them, it acts as a stimulant, ensuring a steady and regular breathing pattern. This natural chemical helps the early rapid breathing rate of a newborn baby to slow down gradually during the first few months and then settle into a breathing rate which is right for life – an important task for every baby.

♥ The instinct to keep your baby close beside you day and night is natural and powerful. So much of what is going on is new and sleeping close beside each other allows your maternal instincts to work well. It helps your sensitive understanding of your baby to grow rapidly. You can watch your baby peacefully and learn his 'language'. He can watch your face to his heart's content.

♥ Your hormones will settle back to normal faster than if you sleep apart from your baby, and 'baby blues' and postnatal depression will be less likely to trouble you.

♥ There is no need to get out of bed or to turn on a light. New medical research findings from all over the world have been collated about the importance of darkness throughout the night for babies and children. Exposure to constant, even low levels of artificial light during the night may reduce levels of melatonin which regulates the body's inner clock. This can lead to restlessness and crying during the night and the day and maybe hyperactivity or other behaviour problems later. An electric light on in the bedroom at night is also known to be one of the causes of the increase in childhood leukaemia and the early onset of short-sightedness.

♥ Switching on a light brings both your and your baby's brain to full alert, making it harder for both of you to get back to sleep quickly. The Bednest makes it as easy as possible to feed, calm and change your baby in the night in total, or almost total, darkness.

♥ You may need to block out street lights with thick, lined curtains or a blanket. A night light, left on just outside the room with the door left a little ajar, will give you just the glimmer of light you need to change your baby's nappy or go to the bathroom yourself.

♥ A child is less likely to grow fearful of the dark if he has slept close enough to his mother during babyhood to smell her, to hear her breathing and to sense her right beside him. The association of these feelings of safety with velvety darkness will still be with him as he grows older.

YOU CAN'T TOUCH A BABY WHO IS OUT OF REACH!

The more a baby, and young children too, are touched lovingly by their parents especially their mother at night, as well as during the day, the better their brain will grow and the calmer and less fearful they will be when they grow up. This will mean less crying and clinging, fewer signs of distress or unkindness. Their sense of peace and safety will have been brought about by your calmness during your pregnancy and the closeness and tenderness of your baby care now.

Reminder: sleeping with your baby in bed with you and/or using a Bednest, or another co-sleeper, will give you hours more sleep every week and therefore more energy. Three mothers describe their experiences:

'It's so much easier and more peaceful to feed a baby in bed, lying down – though I did find it easier sitting up with Tom in bed for the first two weeks when he was still tiny. We all get hours more sleep just slipping him in and out of his Bednest. Feeding him barely wakes me up at all.'

'No more lying awake listening with dread for the first cries of hunger and having to drag myself out of bed and across the room several times each night. No more struggles to settle her down again after a feed, often with my heart thumping while I wait to see if the crying will start up again. No more panic about getting back to sleep myself before half the night has gone!'

'I can respond to him instantly – within seconds – and that is what makes all the difference. I hardly need to lift my head off the pillow.'

Using a co-sleeper like the Bednest helps families to develop a special sense of belonging and sharing – a deep and loving bond. This early closeness also does a great deal to prevent behaviour and relationship problems or aggressive tendencies starting up later in a young child.

Even in the deepest stages of sleep a mother's heightened sensitivity and response to her baby's stirring means she will notice and half-wake to feed when her baby is hungry or she needs to check if he is distressed in any way. This is what Dr James McKenna, one of the best-known American baby care doctors, calls 'sensory vigilance'. It develops rapidly in mothers who bed share or sleep within touch of their infant.

My baby daughter was born by emergency caesarean after a horrendous 16-hour labour. She was distressed and in shock in the hospital and the midwife said that it might take a while for her to calm down because of her birth.

Since we have been home, I have held her constantly in the daytime and at night she sleeps in her Bednest where I can hold her hand and talk softly to her when she whimpers. For the past 5 nights now, she has slept soundly and hasn't cried once. I am convinced this is because she knows I am just a breath away. I think this is an absolutely marvellous product! It has made such a difference to our lives.

One of the best things for us was that Hannah felt so secure after sleeping in a Bednest right beside us for her first 6 months that, when she was moved into her bigger cot on the far side of the room, then into another room next-door, just my voice alone was enough to soothe her when she woke in the night. I didn't need to get out of bed and go to her.

Jo

OTHER CRIBS AND COTS

You may already have a family crib or drop-side cot, or have been lent one by a friend and don't want to use anything else. If this is so, try to work out if there is any way you could safely raise it up so that the edge of the crib or cot is level with your mattress and there is an absolutely secure attachment between the crib or cot and your bed. The important thing to aim for is to be able to lie in bed and see each other's face and for you to be able to reach out and touch your baby at any time during the night.

Wherever your baby sleeps, remember that...

... until your baby is old enough and strong enough to roll over, move around and choose his own favourite sleeping position he should always be laid down to sleep either on his back with his feet against the bottom of the crib or curled up on his left or right side in the familiar, foetal position. These changes in sleeping position are important. They will prevent him developing a flat area at the back of his still soft skull (positional plagiocephaly).

The value of keeping close – in a nutshell

The closer your baby is to you, for the first six to nine months, whether asleep or not, day or night, the happier and safer he will feel.

Babies and young children easily get anxious and fearful if they are put to sleep alone and out of reach, perhaps even out of reach of the sound of your voice. If the sleep time 'memories' of a baby or a young child are of separation and loneliness, primitive alarm bells will go on ringing in his brain in the future. He could find it hard to get to sleep quickly and easily, and stay asleep, even in adulthood. The growth hormone in babies is only released during sleep. Without enough peaceful sleep, his growth and cell repair systems are unable to work as they should.

The main challenge to sort out is that your baby will need more hours of sleep each night than you do. This may mean planning and organising your evening so that your baby can sleep in a sling on your back or in a crib, buggy or pram wherever you are. He will soon learn to sleep as he needs, regardless of family talk, noise and movement around him. Then, when he shows he needs his last feed of the day it will be the right time to go off to bed together for the night.

CHAPTER 10

The Birth

Through the work of brilliant and inspired obstetricians, paediatricians and mother/
baby care specialists, working in the UK, in France and in the USA, we know that babies
are capable of intense feeling – in the womb, during their birth and after their birth. We
understand now, as never before, how much babies sense and 'remember' everything
that happens to them. These 'remembered' feelings are imprinted in every cell in their
bodies, not just in their growing brains.

Birth for every baby is a vast experience. It means being caught up in a tidal wave of
sensations, all new, some exciting, many frightening, some overwhelming.

Your baby can be prepared for his birth and be less overwhelmed by the alarming
pressures and discomforts if you and his dad have been lovingly stroking him through

your skin and talking to him during pregnancy. He will have increasingly heard and sensed the love and welcome in your voices during the last five months.

Every baby's welcome into the world needs to be slow, gentle and full of respect. We need to understand a baby's needs at birth perfectly and help him all we can.

The creative energy and sense of being welcomed into a friendly and loving world your baby will feel for the rest of his life will depend to a surprising degree on the loving welcome, understanding and care he receives before his birth, during his birth and in the first hours and weeks of his life.

In some countries, babies are welcomed through special birth rituals to honour and celebrate childbirth, children and the community. In Burkina Faso villages, a special singing ceremony may take place before each baby is born, assuring them that there are welcoming arms waiting to greet them when they come. *'May the spirit that is in you bring the very many things the world needs for healing.'*

Tibetan communities also reorganise their daily lives round the coming of a new baby – they understand that this is a new spirit coming to teach them.

Achievement and unforgettable joy

YOUR INTUITION

Giving birth will go more easily if you are able to set aside your thinking, calculating mind and slip instead into a state of total absorption. This will show you what your own body and your baby need to complete the birth as naturally as possible, just as all the other animals naturally do.

You need to be 'in a different world' in order to know what positions are best for you during the changing stages of giving birth. The same intuition tells you where and how you need to be held or stroked, when you need silence, or when you need to ask for something else, perhaps a drink of water.

It is instinctive in mothers to try and protect the spirit, the courage and the strength of their baby and themselves as the unbelievable processes of birth engulfs them both.

Sometimes we are not prepared and peaceful enough for our own intuition to work for us. Sometimes we are not prepared for the length of time the birth may take, particularly for a first birth. We may run out of strength and courage and feel like giving up.

A doula or one-to-one midwife with you from beginning to end can transform these feelings by the love and support they give you.

Some mothers have been taught or decide to leave everything to the doctor and midwife. Sometimes, in this case, there is a taking charge and rushing ahead without stopping to ask permission, without respecting the intuitive knowledge birthing mothers have. Mothers usually know if something feels wrong or something different is needed. They need to be listened to and responded to whenever they ask for help.

When our intuition is working, because we are surrounded by kind, unhurried and constant support, giving birth has a healing as well as a creative power that is difficult to describe.

Helping yourself

1. Focus on your breathing – just as you have been practising.

2. Relax your muscles. Gently swaying or rocking, whether standing or sitting, can help to ease tensions in your muscles and release lactic acid.

3. Visualisation – your brain is amazing at diverting your attention. Try imagining yourself in a peaceful place you love.

> *When things were getting really hard to bear towards the second stage of labour, I put my hands on my belly at the end of each contraction and started talking to my baby inside my head. I said things like 'Come on! We can do this together!' 'We'll be OK. Don't panic!' 'Keep going, we're nearly there!' 'Everyone's here to help us.'*

> *Doing this certainly helped me during the hardest part and it somehow made it even more wonderful holding him in my arms when he was born an hour later. The sense that I had kept thinking of him and that we had shared the journey together was a lovely feeling for me afterwards.*
> **Mel**

Birth can be a very sensual experience as a woman moves in rhythm with the energy of all that is going on in her body. In Russia, rhythmic belly dancing is often taught to pregnant women to help them have a more natural birth.

YOUR HORMONES – OXYTOCIN, ENDORPHINS, ADRENALINE

We have all the hormones we need to help us and our baby during the birth. They are ready to hand in our brain and our body, especially if the birth is undisturbed by drugs or medical intervention.

Oxytocin

The word oxytocin comes from the Greek word for 'quick' and 'childbirth labour'. It is a hormone from the pituitary gland which circulates through the blood stream. Rhythmic touch and warmth release oxytocin in us. This is why being stroked, massaged and tenderly kissed is such a comfort and eases your labour.

WHERE IS THE PITUITARY GLAND?

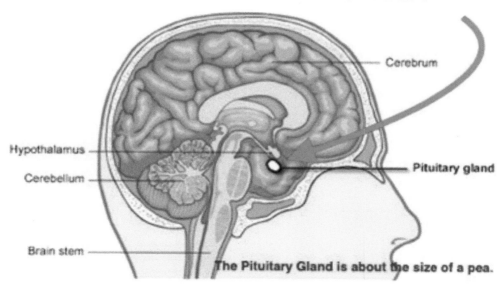

Cerebrum

Hypothalamus

Cerebellum

Pituitary gland

Brain stem

The Pituitary Gland is about the size of a pea.

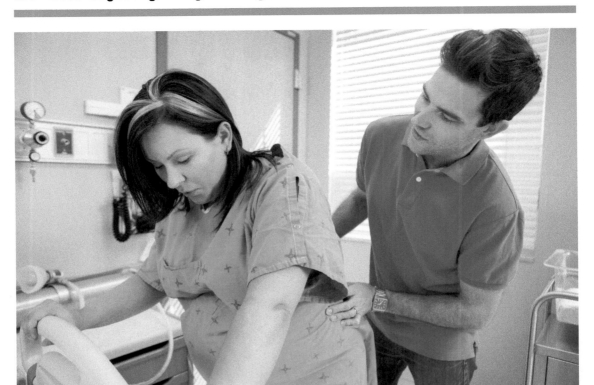

Please massage my back!

The flood of oxytocin allows the horizontal muscles of the uterus to go floppy, which stops holding the baby up in the uterus. It helps the vertical muscles to tighten and so work to nudge the baby down from behind. Oxytocin can cancel out feelings of anger or panic which can cause us to lash out or hide away. It has been there unchanged in humans and animals for millions of years. It reduces bleeding after birth and helps your milk to start flowing.

A mother who feels distressed, unsafe, or unloved during labour may produce low levels of oxytocin. This can cause her contractions to stop and to slow and lengthen labour. The response to this is invariably medical intervention, which may add to her tension.

Oxytocin is sometimes called 'the cuddle hormone' because it goes on and on working to help us. When your baby starts to cry, more oxytocin is released. When your baby sucks that also activates the release of oxytocin. This has a calming effect on you. You can almost feel it happening. All warm human bonds are fed by oxytocin.

Endorphins

Endorphins are calming and pain-relieving hormones which are produced in response to hard physical work, stress or pain. It is the high endorphin levels in you, during labour and birth, which produce an altered state of consciousness. This helps you flow with the process, even if the birth is long and arduous. Endorphins can help you, despite the hard work of labour and birth, to feel alert, attentive and even euphoric immediately after the birth and as you begin to care for your baby. They help you to fall in love with each other.

If you can be helped to stay calm and confident during labour and birth, and be protected from disturbances, unwelcome people or noise, the production of endorphins in you will increase.

Epidurals or opioids (drugs) given as pain relief will prevent your body from producing endorphins.

Adrenaline

Adrenaline is our 'fight or flight' survival hormone. It is released into the bloodstream when we feel threatened. Mothers who do not feel safe and protected may produce high levels of adrenaline during labour.

The constant release of adrenaline can slow labour or stop it altogether. Thousands of years ago, this made it possible for women giving birth to be moved away from danger to a place of safety.

As your baby travels through the birth canal, his body begins to produce two hormones: adrenaline and noradrenaline. Adrenaline prepares him for the enormous change to breathing air. It opens up his lungs and dries their dampness. Noradrenaline works to slow his heartbeat towards the end of labour. This helps him to manage without much oxygen reaching him from the umbilical cord during the actual birth.

WHAT DOES YOUR BABY NEED MOST?

Because babies' heads are so big in proportion to their bodies they have to be born through that narrow pelvic pathway some months before they are really developed enough to be ready for the outside world. They are born far more frail and defenceless and far less physically competent than any other mammal. They take longer to grow up and need devoted attention and care as they develop.

These, then, are a baby's first and greatest needs during the birth:

♥ That his mother feels safe, protected and lovingly cared for throughout the birth. She needs privacy and quiet with one-to-one, unhurried and trusted support. The only hurrying that should ever happen is if there is an emergency and she needs urgent medical help.

♥ That his mother is encouraged to follow her own instincts, to move about and to ask for the kind of help she feels she needs – and is given it. The buoyancy of a warm bath can increase relaxation and mobility and reduce discomfort.

♥ That his mother is helped to slow down and go into her own world with as little interruption and talk as possible. She needs encouragement to keep moving and trying all the different positions... standing... kneeling... on hands and knees... squatting... leaning forward onto someone or onto a chair or against the wall. Gravity is a big help. These partly instinctive and partly learned skills can ease things along and are kindest to a baby. The blood circulates more freely, carrying oxygen to the baby and to the muscles of the uterus.

♥ That his mother is encouraged to breathe steadily and not to hold her breath until the time has come to push him out. If her jaw and throat are relaxed, so will relaxation come more easily with the pelvis and birth canal.

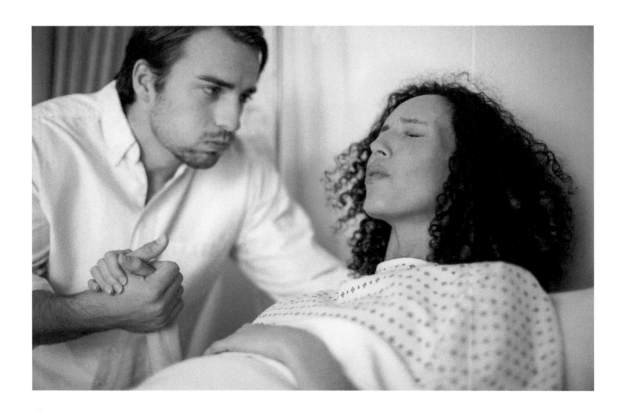

♥ That the lights are dimmed in time for the birth – or the curtains are drawn if the birth is at home – so that he is not blinded by coming straight out of darkness into the shock of dazzling light the first time he opens his eyes. Over the first couple of months a baby's eyes need to be protected from bright light so that they do not hurt but have time to adjust, slowly.

♥ That his acute sense of hearing is understood and respected, not shattered by the louder, sharper sounds of the outside world – especially the loud noises in a hospital. What a baby has been hearing in the womb is dim and muted compared to what he hears after birth, due to the water surrounding him and his mother's body, acting as a double sound barrier. At birth he could be facing an explosion of sound unless everyone in the room remembers that this would be a further stress for him to bear. To be welcomed into a loving silence with all words spoken with muted voices or in a whisper for the next hour or so will protect him from another source of tension. His ears are given time to become acclimatised slowly to the sudden, new and stronger sounds around him. There will be no sudden shocks to startle him and make all his muscles jerk.

Labour

We talked together about Ellie finding a picture in her mind to use to encourage her during labour - perhaps even have a photograph to look at now and again.
Ellie's midwife

I wanted to imagine myself like a flower opening up in the sun.
I can remember Pete looking steadily into my eyes whenever my eyes were open during contractions! It gave me something warm and loving to focus on. It helped me to slow myself down so I could sense what position I wanted to be in. It also helped me to have a 'yes!' feeling with each contraction instead of 'no more, I've had enough!'
Sometimes during the labour Pete kissed me on the lips as if we were making love - just as a big contraction started up. It sounds mad but it did something wonderful - it made the final pushing more exciting than painful.
Ellie

We hardly spoke through the last three hours of labour. The midwife only smiled encouragement and answered my questions quietly and quickly – nothing more. I knew Ellie needed to get right into the instinctive, primitive, wordless part of her brain and stay there without any distractions. We just talked to each other with our eyes. Whenever I felt a bit stressed from watching her struggling all on her own I turned away and looked out of the window for a moment. There was a tree outside and the sky beyond it.

The best thing anyone could ever have said to me was: 'remember that your baby loves you more than anything you can imagine, even right now in the middle of the struggles to be born'. That was Ellie's midwife again. She was wonderful to both of us and it is as if her spirit and understanding are still with us now.

Ellie's husband, Pete

> *I learnt to help Aika to keep moving as long as she could. I learnt to help her change from one position to the other as her instinct told her. I was her 'leaning post' all through the first stage when she wanted to walk and move around. Sometimes I held her head against me; sometimes I stroked her neck or rubbed her back or her legs. I kissed the top of her head and her hands. I gave her sips of water when she pointed at the glass. We had planned that she would tell me what helped and what didn't. I found myself watching out for her little nods and head shakes when she didn't want to say even one word to anyone while all her attention had to be on the great effort going on just below her heart.*
> **Daniel**

The birth

The squeezing and the pressures forcing your baby down the birth canal, so different from the peace and comfort of the womb, give him a great surge of adrenaline. It is this adrenaline racing around his little body that helps him to start breathing as soon as he is born, to search for your face and then discover how to suck with his lips and his tongue. This surge of adrenaline usually makes a newborn baby wonderfully alert, often gazing and gazing into your eyes as if he is searching you out. We call this time 'the Magic Window'. You can read more about it in the next section.

If he is with you, hand your baby as soon as possible to his dad to hold.

> *It's impossible to describe the flood of emotion that hit me when I held her in my arms, ten minutes old, and started talking to her. Almost at once she was looking straight into my eyes. She locked herself to me with her eyes. It was like: 'Oh! There you are!' and all I could think was: 'Mine! mine! mine! – And she knows it!'*
> **Jonno**

Let time stand still

When a baby has been born and laid on his mother's tummy, the first and most important thing is to do nothing at all. To wait. To be still. To be quiet. To let five slow minutes go by at least. Your baby still has a foot in two worlds and he needs time to adjust with no interference or interruption. Lying now, warm and safe on his mother's now flatter belly, he can slowly settle into breathing on his own, without feeling alarmed by these astonishing new sensations... until his heart and lungs have taken over entirely from the umbilical cord... as it ceases to pulse. Do nothing. Just wait. Enjoy the tiny in-and-out breathing movements of his whole back and watch him begin to reach out with his hands to feel your skin. Wait for a leg to begin to move and kick.

In these ways your baby's birth will become more like a peaceful awakening and discovery instead of a series of shocks.

> *A newborn baby should never be laid flat on his back immediately after the birth to check anything because, in a single spasm, his spine, which has been curved for so long, would be straightened. A baby must be able to uncoil his spine and stretch his back at his own pace.*
> **Dr Frédérick Leboyer**

To see beautiful examples and amazing photographs of babies born in silence and love, with him in attendance, see *Birth Without Violence* by Dr Frédérick Leboyer (especially page 114).

> https://embryo.asu.edu/pages/birth-without-violence-1975-frederick-leboyer
> www.liddlekidz.com Infant massage and touch therapy

Wherever your baby is born it helps to know how easy it is for you yourself to avoid early problems by keeping your baby lying skin-to-skin for as long as possible across your chest. A too high breathing rate can easily be lowered by helping your baby to suckle immediately.

Even a baby needing resuscitation can remain on your belly while this is done and not have to suffer the extra stress of being taken away from you.

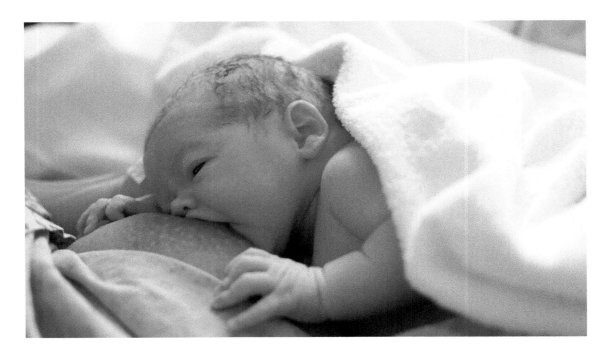

THE MAGIC WINDOW – TOUCH AND CLOSENESS

There is often a magic window in that first half an hour after birth when the adrenaline is still flowing in your baby and he is unbelievably wide awake; when he feels his own breath filling him and your hands touching him; when he begins to gaze entranced at your face; when he starts to move and smell your milk and reach instinctively for your breast – and start sucking. He seems so completely alert and wise and shows this to you so clearly before falling into a deep and exhausted sleep. This is the reward to bring you joy to add to your relief. Not to be missed, not to be hurried and never to be forgotten.

Your first meeting with your baby

A dim light also helps a mother begin to bond with her baby naturally and easily. It means that the first meeting will be as much through slow and tender touch as through gazing at each other. Through a hand, lightly laid on his back, she will sense the peace that her baby is beginning to feel – in the warm nest of her belly as it rises and falls with the rhythm of her breathing. He feels the security, too, of finding himself close to her heart once more.

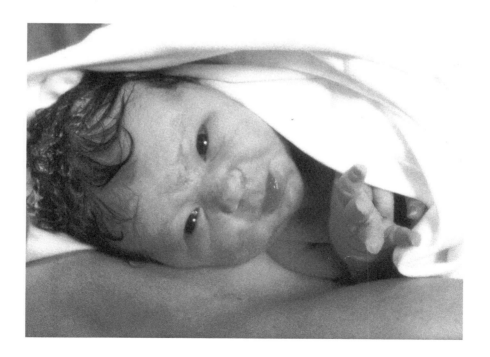

When a baby has been protected by loving voices and touch while still in the womb (whenever there have been times of anxiety, sadness or anger) and when there is gentleness and joy at his welcome, then it becomes more than a birth. It becomes a 'blessed' event, inspiring everyone who is there.

Frédérick Leboyer describes the effect on a baby of his being lowered into a warm bath right beside his mother an hour or two after his birth. It's like being back in the womb, cradled by two big hands, weightless again in the warm water and floating free.

> *He starts to explore... he starts to move every way he can. He turns one way, then the other, twisting as far as his neck allows. His hands open and close, reach out, feel the space, find each other. One moves away, the other reaches after it. A foot shoots out, pushing against the edge of the bath. Then does it again. He has started to play. Every inch of him is moving. His mouth opens and closes. His tongue flickers. His hand finds his lips. His taste for adventure will always be with him after such a start.*

Touch and closeness are vital for the first few months

♥ The sound of his mother's heart beating is so familiar and comforting to a baby before birth that a newborn needs to lie across his mother's chest or be held in her arms for as many hours a day as possible during those first few weeks. When a baby is separated from his mother he pines for her 'body sounds', even when he appears to be sleeping peacefully. Most mothers anywhere in the world instinctively hold their babies on the left side where the sound of their heartbeat is strongest.

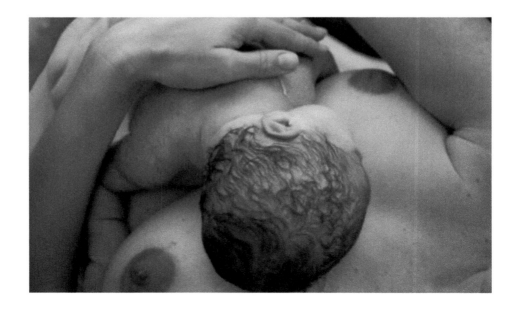

The vibration of that steady sound, 70-80 beats a minute, helps to regulate a baby's breathing and heart rate, as well as calming him. A calm baby makes his mother calm in the same way that a calm mother brings calm to her baby. What do we have long, strong arms for? Why do mothers all over the world put their baby in a sling on their chest or on their back? Babies who lie right across their mother's or their father's chest sleep in absolute bliss. It's the best place of all.

♥ Babies have a perfect sense of smell and start to recognise their mother's smell with their first breath, if they are not moved away from her but can lie on her the moment they are born. A newborn baby will smell her milk, her skin, her breath and in no time will be able to tell the difference between her smell and the smell of anyone else holding him. A baby will learn his own father's smell as quickly if he is held and carried by him from birth.

The smell of each other!

A newborn baby laid down in a crib or pram to sleep will be comforted by having an unwashed shirt or vest from his mother stretched over his mattress. His sense of separation is lessened.

If the birth has been difficult, healing and recovery will start for him if you carry him in your arms as much as possible, skin-to-skin kangaroo care, and by stroking, cuddling, kissing, talking, crooning and humming to him. Big smiles whenever he is awake and alert will do more than anything to make him feel safe, loved and glad to be alive.

Memories

Newborn babies remember in all kinds of ways. Memories are imprinted in their brain, in their nerve endings and in all the cells of their body, especially in their skin cells. For example, a baby who has had a heel punctured for a blood sample just after birth will cry months later if you grip that same foot suddenly. The memory is in his cells and his nervous system.

If a baby's breathing is accidentally stopped by his whole face being squashed against a full breast he will remember this slightly scary experience and may be breast shy for a short while, even if he is only a day or two old.

Later on, young children can, out of the blue, remember and sing a song or say a phrase that they heard time and again while they were still in the womb. They are like sponges, soaking up words, phrases and music even before they were born.

However old we are, we ourselves can remember the good feelings we had in the womb. A good womb feeling can come back to any of us at any time, perhaps when

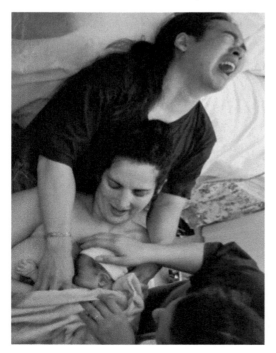

walking by the sea, being enclosed in a beautiful place, sitting in a sunny garden or curling up in bed. If our time in the womb was not so safe and happy, perhaps because our mother was feeling distressed or helpless at that time, we may be left with unexplainable stabs of sadness or anger or fear as we grow up. We may even feel uneasiness about seas, mountains, forests and wide-open spaces. We may feel a need to keep our lives 'little' and unadventurous in order to feel safe.

This man had experienced near suffocation and great fear at his own birth. He now found it almost intolerable, worrying about the birth of his own child. He had no idea why he had been feeling so distressed throughout the pregnancy but it was almost certainly that the buried memories of his own birth were overwhelming him again. The midwife knew about this and gave him support and help with his feelings throughout the labour. He gave a great cry and wept with joy and relief as his baby was born. He was the first to hold her. All those long-buried and terrifying memories faded away at last.

Premature babies

Very, very rarely and distressingly a premature baby can seem so scary and strange in appearance that his parents are overwhelmed by the stress and worry of watching him in such a frail and passive state. Their instinct to love and protect him may be frozen by their present feelings and by their fears for the future. Whenever this happens these parents will be given continuous comfort, encouragement and emotional support from experienced neonatal nurses while they learn how to handle their baby in ways that will help their confidence to grow and turn into tenderness and devotion. Kangaroo care, skin-to-skin, chest-to-chest contact between Mum and baby and Dad and baby, as soon as that is possible and for as long as possible every day, helps most of all. This gives premature babies the best chance to start to thrive and catch up. When your baby is strong enough to come home it is ideal to have him sleeping close beside you in a Bednest, within sight, smell and touch of you all night and able to feed without disturbance as many times as needed.

A CD of lullabies called *Music for Dreaming*, created by Cherie Ross and the Melbourne Symphony Orchestra, has been shown to give great comfort and peace to

mothers as well as to premature or distressed babies. The flute, strings and harp recreate the continuous, comforting and familiar sounds of the womb and echo the rhythm of the resting heartbeat.

www.musicfordreaming.com/moreinfo-1.html

Soon after the birth

Bedtime story. Back to normal, four hours after a home birth.

Keeping close to older children and your newborn baby so you all belong to each other from the very beginning is calming and comforting. It also helps to prevent jealousy causing problems.

It's a good idea to talk through your birth experience afterwards with someone who was there with you during the labour and birth. You can together judge how much any moment of feeling overwhelmed and panicked could have distressed your baby and talk about the ways which can help to soothe him when he cries. The best way of all is to talk to yourself and to your baby calmly, to do everything slowly and gently throughout each day with your baby in a sling or close beside you, and to lie down whenever you can with your baby across your chest or on your stomach, skin-to-skin. There is nothing more healing for both of you than this. Humming quietly to your baby is calming too, so is a shared bath and so is being out of doors in a green and peaceful place.

A baby's time in the womb and birth experience together can lay down a pattern of how he will feel and behave for the rest of his life. A close and loving bond and warm feelings of security and delight between a mother and her baby are the foundation for *every* future relationship her child will have.

Mothers who can't love their babies

Very occasionally, a mother is so shaken up by sad and harmful memories, or a difficult and exhausting birth, that she finds herself feeling indifferent towards her baby after the birth. Also, this can happen if a mother has herself been neglected when she was a baby. It is of huge importance that this is noticed at once, and that she is given experienced understanding, comfort and help immediately and continuously as she learns the skills of baby care until a loving bond starts to grow.

There are many ways to help these mothers and there are people with professional training to do this (see Appendices 2, 3 and 4).

> *I didn't even want to look at my baby at first. When she was born she seemed like an alien. It was as if she didn't belong to me. I just lay there, feeling scared and upset and somehow angry and guilty too. It was terrible.*
>
> *My partner was wonderful. He held the baby and carried her around and talked to her for hours and hours that first week. He kept talking to me too, telling me all about her while I sat on the sofa feeling sorry for myself. Gradually, listening to him began to help me and I started holding her for a few minutes after feeds and watching her little pouting face. I was given so much unfussed support and encouragement it turned everything round for us. Now I have a cheeky and wonderful 2 year old and can hardly bear to be apart from her.*
> **A first-time mum**

The best possible – in a nutshell

♥ When a mother has been surrounded by kindness, patience and support and given privacy and peace during the birth...

♥ When her baby has been welcomed by soft and unhurried hands and cocooned by near darkness and gentle murmurs at the moment of birth...

♥ When he has been laid immediately on the warm, soft skin of his mother's stomach with the umbilical cord left pulsing to continue to feed oxygen to him while he learns to start breathing steadily himself...

When these three things have been there for him, he should have no need to cry, except perhaps for his first few out-breaths. He will soon be yawning and stretching and trying to focus his eyes on his mother's face with amazing concentration. We can watch this marvellous thing happening before our very eyes and feel peace and joy filling the room.

All these ways of welcoming a baby into the world will help to dissolve the fear, the distress and even moments of panic that he may have suffered at some time during the birth – when there has been no way for you to reach and comfort him.

We may think there has been no way to reach and comfort him but, of course, there is still your voice. Talking softly and lovingly to your baby, when you have breath for it, during the birth, *will* reach him and *will* comfort him. It may also steady you because it reminds you that you are 'in it together'.

This is a picture of the very best. However, not all of it may have worked out as you hoped for one reason or another. Try not to feel upset or anxious if your plans and hopes for your birth have not been completely realised. The understanding and the wisdom behind these birthing ways will stay with you and you will still be able to use this understanding as you care for your growing baby or if you become pregnant again.

IF a baby dropz out of
your tummy when your
zhopping You muzt ring
the police.

Deborah Age 6

CHAPTER 11

Breastfeeding

YOUR BABY KNOWS BEST

In the natural way of things your baby is full of adrenaline just after the birth and will be alert and wide awake for that first hour. This is what is called the Magic Window. He will gaze and gaze at your face and quite soon will show signs of trying to creep, inch by inch, up your belly towards your breast. He will bob his head until he finds one of your nipples and, with mouth opening and closing, will try to latch on and start to suck. This is his natural reflex. It works perfectly if you are lying flat after the birth with one hand supporting his bottom.

There should be stillness and peace in the room and no hurry or interruption for as long as possible.

YOUR MILK IS FANTASTIC!

When you are a baby your mother feeds you from her boZom but she can only do milk.

Felicity Aged 7

In your milk there are twenty different hormonal substances to help your baby's digestive system, to encourage the growth of his intestines and his ability to absorb the nutrients in your milk. The best start for both of you! With each breastfeeding you also feel more inseparably connected to him – which is what he needs just as much as he needs your milk. Surprisingly, frequent breastfeeding lessens the chances of getting sore nipples.

Your milk, particularly the rich colostrum which comes first, contains antibodies against salmonella and many other potentially dangerous viruses and bacteria in the environment. This is why it is worth taking all the time and trouble needed to express milk for him if you ever have to be separated for some reason during the first hours, days or weeks.

When he is sucking at your breast your brain is stimulated to produce the hormones which in turn stimulate your breasts to produce more milk. A healthy, full-term baby should lead the way, especially during the night when he has you all to himself with no interruptions. The frequency and completion of his sucking at night is very important. Your milk is richer then and his regular suckling during the night will ensure that you continue to produce exactly the right amount of milk he needs as he grows.

> *Make sure your baby's nose and toes are facing the same way so she doesn't need to twist her head to feed.*
> **A midwife in Manchester**

Breastfeeding reduces stress in your baby and in you. It lifts your mood and will help to protect you from postnatal depression. It also protects your baby from any harmful effects even when you are feeling stressed or depressed yourself for a while. This is why it is so important to get help quickly and sort any breastfeeding problems you have.

Other things that can help you

Three natural supplements: EPA (eicosapentaenoic acid), DHA (docasahexaenoic acid), St John's Wort

1. Taking increasing exercise each day, in green spaces if possible, as you recover from the birth
2. Talking about your sad thoughts and feelings with someone you trust as well as with your midwife, if possible without any delay, not even for a day
3. These proven methods will help you to avoid 'baby blues' and postnatal depression.

They come from Kathleen Kendall-Tackett PhD, IBCLC, FAPA.
www.kathleenkendall-tackett.com/Articles-depression.html

THE UNICEF BABY FRIENDLY INITIATIVE

Unicef is the world's leading organisation for children, working in over ninety countries. The Baby Friendly Initiative is a worldwide programme to improve the standard of care to mothers and babies and also to encourage and support breastfeeding, with a strong emphasis on helping mothers to breastfeed successfully. The Baby Friendly Initiative also works to help to build strong parent-child relationships.

Unicef research shows us that breastfeeding helps protect your baby against:

- Ear infections
- Asthma
- Chest infections
- Gastro-intestinal infections
- Urine infections
- Obesity
- Childhood diabetes
- Breast cancer, ovarian cancer and weak bones later in life

Find out more about Unicef UK and how the Baby Friendly Initiative supports new parents at www.unicef.org.uk/babyfriendly

Contact at bfi@unicef.org.uk

TO MAKE LIFE AS EASY AS POSSIBLE FOR EVERY MUM

The more time you can spend in skin-to-skin contact with your baby, immediately after the birth and when carrying him in a sling in the first days and weeks, the easier it will be to breastfeed successfully. Your milk production will increase as your growing baby needs more and sucks more strongly. It is especially important to sleep very close to each other at night, perhaps using an attached bedside crib. You will be able to feed him as often as he needs without having to switch on a light or get out of bed. It is the night feeds which are the richest and which will set the pattern for his growing milk needs, month by month.

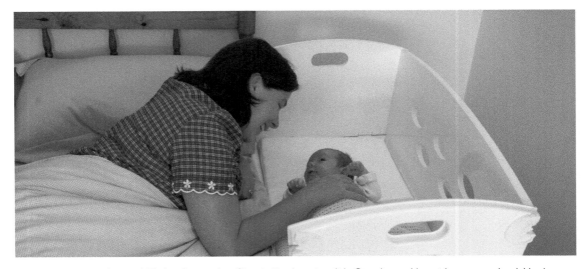

The first, marketed Right from the Start Bednest with Sarah and her three-week-old baby.
Just the right distance between their faces for him to see her beautiful smile.

The understanding between you and your baby will grow rapidly with skin-to-skin contact – with every touch between you at night as well as during the day. It will also prevent a build-up of crying and fussing.

There *are* reasons why breastfeeding your baby, especially your first baby, may take a little while to establish:

- He might be so exhausted after the birth that the need to sleep is greater than the need to suck.

- If he has been separated from you, even for twenty minutes, for weighing, washing or checking, he will lose his instinct to creep up unaided, find your breast and start sucking. He will need help to find the way. Even short times of separation should never happen unless there are urgent medical reasons to do so.

- If you have had drugs or medical intervention of any kind, before or during the birth, his alertness may be reduced and his instincts dulled. He will need to be held and talked to quietly for as long as possible.

- Sore nipples can mean sharp pain to be endured at the beginning of each feed. This can be quite distressing, especially while you are still learning to get him in the right position against your breast and your nipple far enough back in his mouth. The best soothing and healing cream to use after each feed seems to be Lansinoh but your midwife may have another suggestion. This should put things right within a few days.

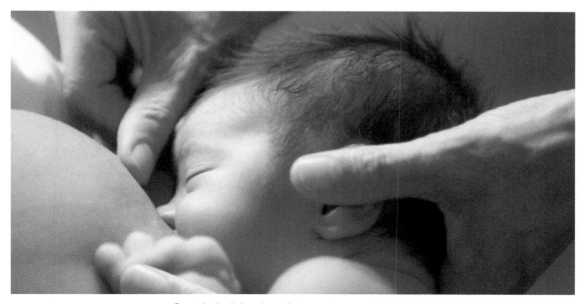

Gentle, helping hands to get you started

If the birth has been very hard and scary for him, maybe he will be feeling too tired and shocked to look for your face? He will need recovery time with skin-to-skin contact, loving touch, stillness, your quietest voice, near darkness and sleep until he begins to recover. He may even need some medical support for a short while but this is rare. Try not to feel sad or anxious, the Magic Window and sucking will just come a little later.

THINGS TO UNDERSTAND

When you breastfeed, the milk comes flooding out of its own accord at first. Then, after about six weeks, it can suddenly seem to be much less, so that the baby has to suck harder and really work for it. This could be because you are not resting and drinking enough but it mainly happens because of hormone changes in you. There is a reason for this. Your baby needs to begin, even at this early stage in his life, to take responsibility and do his best. He has to build his character and inner strength. Therefore, don't feel anxious when there seems suddenly to be less milk. This is part of a natural process. It happens at this time because it takes more or less six weeks for a baby to adjust to being born and to all the new experiences in her life.

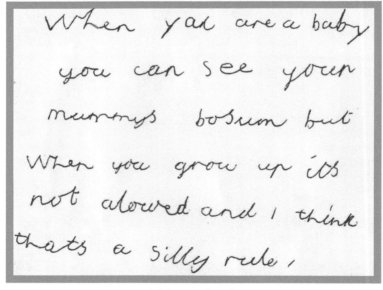

When you are a baby you can see your mummys bosum but when you grow up its not alowed and i think thats a silly rule.

Vivienne Age 6

Very important!

Neither you nor he should have to concentrate on anything else but each other. Everything should be as easy and peaceful as possible for you, with no other demands. You need your husband, partner or anyone else who is looking after you to protect you from an invasion of visitors or any other distraction for the first six weeks.

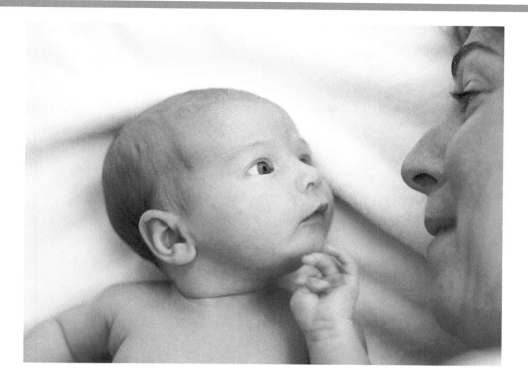

Hormone changes in you

When your baby cries when he feeds, it may be because he senses the hormone changes. He may be feeling slight stomach cramps caused by the doubtful feeling that is coming to him with these changes in you. By keeping calm and letting him suck for longer and more often, especially at night, he will quickly return to normal. When there has been a need to adjust like this, it may take time for your mind to calm down, and his little brain too.

To help a baby who is easily distracted from sucking by other things going on around her, try tenting him for a while under your shirt or a shawl over your shoulders.

Unable to breastfeed?

Having said all that, if you cannot breastfeed because of the medication you are on or for some other good reason it is really very important to accept this and to relax. Baby formulas get closer to the real thing all the time as the scientists work on them. Get expert advice about which brand would be best for your baby and do your best to stop worrying anymore about it.

If you are unable to breastfeed, for whatever reason, it is especially important to sleep within touch of each other; this is always the case with an adopted baby. This will be like a lifeline for your baby and make up for the slightly separating effect of drinking from a bottle. It is not too difficult to organise a way to warm up a bottle beside your bed for night feeds in a very dim light, sleeping close so you don't need to get up and go to the kitchen, leaving your baby alone just when he is waking and needing you.

> *I was really upset when I realised that I was not going to be able to breastfeed my baby after all. What helped me most was doing relaxation exercises, listening to my favourite music and thinking of all the mothers in the world whose babies actually die because there is no formula milk available for them. I realised how lucky I was.*
> **Kimberly**

Cluster feeding

Some babies when they are a month or two old begin to want to suckle on and off all evening with barely a gap in between feeds. Your baby may be thrashing about and crying most evenings, sometimes for a distressingly long time. He won't settle to sleep. This can be stressful for you and quite a problem if you have to interrupt feeding and calming him to take care of someone else or something else.

If he demands cluster feeding, it is his own best instinct at work. He needs to suckle more at the end of the day, partly because your milk has become less rich and sustaining by the evening and partly to get every drop of the 'hindmilk' because this is what will help him get to sleep and then sleep deeply and for longer during the night.

How to cope

What possible preparations could you make to organise things in advance of your baby's cluster-feeding time? Getting everything ready for the evening meal? Bathing a toddler earlier than usual and having him ready for bed in his pyjamas? Could you re-arrange things enough to enjoy cluster-feeding time by being free to relax, talk, read to an older child or watch a nature or children's programme or a DVD?

Or just stop, do nothing. Sit, drink anything but alcohol. Sipping a glass of water slowly can help you calm down. Eat a treat slowly. Cuddle rock and suckle your baby until he calms down. Some babies are calmed by being held heart-to-heart and going walkabout.

Your baby's need to cluster feed will gradually lessen and your evenings will be less in danger of being hectic and stressful.

The need to suck

Because the action of sucking has a calming effect on your baby, you may want to give him a pacifier at sleep times and bedtime just to help him settle peacefully to sleep during the first year – when you may be suffering from a shortage of sleep yourself. However, it is best not to start this until he is a month old and breastfeeding is going well.

A premature baby's brain will develop better if he can be breastfed instead of being given formula milk. The eyes of breastfed babies develop faster and a baby born jaundiced or shocked by the birth will recover quickly if he's breastfed frequently – ten or eleven times in twenty-four hours. This may mean just an hour or so between one short sucking and the next during the day and slightly longer spaces at night until you can see he is recovering.

Crying immediately after a feed?

Some mothers find themselves feeling concerned when their breastfed baby sometimes becomes unsettled and cries soon after a feed and fills their nappy with a watery 'poo'. This is only very rarely caused by lactose intolerance (difficulties in digesting milk properly). The discomfort and crying is much more likely to be caused by a failure to *finish* the first breast and therefore take in the high-fat hindmilk (the best bit) that comes later in the feed. This hindmilk balances with the first flow (more of a thirst quencher). It makes digestion easier and helps your baby to feel comfortable and satisfied.

Solution: Stick to one breast at a time and don't worry about being lopsided. Don't move to the second breast until the flow has stopped in the first. As your baby gets older, stronger and hungrier, he'll probably suck both dry in no time and may still ask for more. You may need to check and keep checking that you are drinking enough and regularly (anything except caffeinated drinks and alcohol); also doing all you can to eat fresh, whole foods at every meal and snack.

When I was pregnant, I tried my best to eat healthy food, especially fruit and veg and to eat regularly. My midwife told me that my baby would have to adapt himself to grow as best he could, even with a shortage of one important nutrient or another and that this shortage in the womb might delay his full and healthy growth. It could perhaps lead to serious health problems later in his life. I wouldn't want that.

I would have died a death without my midwife. When I was pregnant, she watched over me and she noticed when I was getting really worried and upset two weeks after the birth. She saw me or talked on the telephone almost every day until I felt better.
Niki

We'd all be better off if there were many more midwives and health visitors who could give us help with our emotions, as well as teach us what we should be eating and how to get fit for the birth. I only saw my midwife after the birth for five minutes at a time and I never had a visit from a health visitor. I was told to ring up and ask for a visit if I wanted one – but you don't do that, do you, to someone you haven't even met?
Noor

Love hormones

The French obstetrician Michel Odent used the term 'love hormones' to describe the release of oxytocin and endorphins that make you feel good, perhaps even 'high'. They are released during love making and orgasm, during labour, just after the birth and during breastfeeding.

Oxytocin is also the 'mothering hormone' setting off intense feelings of love and closeness to your baby. Prolactin, the hormone released during breastfeeding, also awakens your mothering instinct. These two hormones, together with the oestrogen and progesterone from the placenta, are in high concentration and they, too, push aside the rational workings of your brain and give extra stimulus to your loving and mothering feelings.

'Off to the best start': This Unicef Baby Friendly Initiative booklet (published in collaboration with the NHS) is full of helpful breastfeeding photographs and instructions. It is outstanding.

www.unicef.org.uk/babyfriendly/baby-friendly-resources/breastfeeding-resources/off-to-the-best-start/

If you need more help, talk to your midwife or health visitor or contact one of these breastfeeding helplines:

NCT
0870 444 8708
www.nct.org.uk

The Breastfeeding Network
0870 900 8787
www.breastfeedingnetwork.org.uk

La Leche League
0845 120 2918
www.laleche.org.uk

Association of Breastfeeding Mothers
0870 401 7711
www.abm.me.uk

~ CHAPTER 12 ~

After the Birth

Being touched and caressed, being massaged, is food for the infant; food as necessary as minerals, vitamins, and proteins. Deprived of this food, the name of which is love, babies would rather die.
Frédérick Leboyer, French obstetrician, author of Birth Without Violence. **This includes the photograph below of a baby, just born, lovingly held and almost smiling.**

RECOVERY

The first few days after the birth of your baby is a time like no other. It is different for every mum and every dad but there is always one thing in common: this is the need to have peaceful, undisturbed and unhurried time together to touch, to stroke, to hold and to watch your baby and to talk to each other… and to sleep.

From the moment your baby is born, stillness, quiet, skin-to-skin touch and smiling faces are what matter most. These essential comforts during the next two hours at least – and then as often and for as long as possible every day – will do more than anything else to help you settle down as a new family.

Mothers, especially during the first few weeks, need protection from interruptions and distractions. They need to be loved, supported and calmed to recover from the struggles of giving birth and to allow their hormones to rebalance. They also need help and companionship for the tasks of learning how to feed and care for their baby during the night as well as the day and how to soothe him without becoming anxious every time he cries.

The main priority when your baby is born is feelings of calm, delight and safety. If instead you find yourself frequently feeling alone, anxious and distressed, *help and comfort* for you must be found from someone, quickly – like food for someone who is starving.

Appendix 2: Recovering from a Hard Birth may help you.

GO WALKABOUT... TALKABOUT

The best way to get yourself talking in a normal, everyday adult way to your baby is to begin as soon as he has been born and you can walk around with him in your arms. This is the perfect time to start explaining this and that to him and sharing happy thoughts with him. It shows your respect for his hidden intelligence. If he was born in hospital this is his first homecoming. It is an amazing moment for you and for him.

Perhaps you will want first to sit with a cup of tea, and feed him or both sleep for a while, to let the familiarity of your own home come back to you and the excitement die down a little. If you had a home birth you can just choose your own time to introduce him to his own home and everything in it. You may then decide to treat him as if he was a very distinguished and special guest and give him a tour. Show and share with him in your own way and in your own words some things of interest in each room where you live.

Talk slowly and quietly and move slowly and gently. Carry him around, telling him about anything your eye falls on:

'Look! This is where we sleep... there's our bed... the carpet is pink and grey... and there are your dad's trainers in the middle of it... out of the window I can see bushes and there's the cat next door licking its back leg... now I'll show you the bathroom... look, two different kinds of toothpaste!... this is where we do the cooking... this is the kitchen sink... I'll turn on the tap so you can hear the water running!... and this is our bath. It's a bit too big for you just now but we'll be able to put you in it when you're older. I've got a little bath for you much smaller than this... look here it is!... that's the toilet and it flushes. I bet you'll enjoy the noise it makes.' Just use your own eyes and your own ideas and imagination!

All this might seem like madness, but think about it for a moment and you will realise how much it will help you to get into a natural habit of sharing thoughts and feelings, as well as respecting his intelligence and understanding as he grows. And he will get the feel of, and understand, what you are talking about so rapidly you will hardly believe it!

Babies are brilliant at remembering and learning

Your baby, if he has not been shocked and exhausted by his birth and retreated into himself for a few days to recover, will start to turn his head to follow your voice and face within about four days. But he will need your face to be very close, because his ability to focus is only about 30cm.

When there have been no anaesthetics during the labour and birth, babies will start to watch their parents' faces very carefully. They even start to copy expressions and movements in the first few days, sticking out their tongue, opening their mouth wide. They are 'inspection scanning' whenever they are awake and alert, from the moment of birth. If we watch carefully enough we can see this love of learning in their behaviour already, and how carefully they try to focus.

Dr T. Berry Brazelton is an American paediatrician who wanted to understand what very young babies are telling us by their behaviour. He watched thousands of babies from birth to two months old very closely, and noticed that they can communicate their likes and dislikes from birth. Babies are very fast learners, so helping them stay calm means that they will have quiet, alert times when they will be able to learn and understand what is going on around them. The quicker we come to understand what our baby is feeling, showing us and 'telling' us, the sooner he will feel settled and secure.

Mothers should hold their babies close. Fathers should take them to the highest hill and show them how wide and wonderful the world is.
Dr T. Berry Brazelton

He will turn his head towards your familiar voice or his father's familiar voice – even within a few hours of birth. He will ignore the voice of a stranger. When he is alert and awake, he will follow a bright object with his eyes and his head if you move it slowly across his line of sight.

All this shows you how intelligent and capable your baby is and how much he has already learned and remembered and held in his head and his heart from the beginning.

Real playfulness between parents and babies begins from two months old but the shadow of a smile can be visible on a baby's face within an hour of birth. Twins often smile more and earlier than babies born singly. They have probably been playing with each other in the womb. Early smiles like these are only partial smiles. They don't reach the muscles round a baby's eyes and forehead.

LOVING TOUCH MATTERS ALL OUR LIVES

It is through our hands that we speak to the child. That we communicate. Touch is the child's first language, understanding comes long after feeling.
Frédérick Leboyer

Touch is our first longing. It 'speaks' without the use of words. It is also the last sense to leave us when we die.

When we talk about 'being touched' by something we see happening or something someone has said or done, we are talking about a 'heart' feeling. Babies and toddlers live through their sensations, so touch and soothing sounds may be the only language they can understand for a while.

Babies are hungry for touch from the moment they are born. Touching, stroking and skin-to-skin contact with your baby – and the more the better – is perfection. Boy babies seem to need this tender touch even more than girl babies.

Gentle stroking of your baby's skin with your fingertips or the palm of your hand... rubbing... kissing all over... cuddling... hand-holding... foot-holding... and stroking over his forehead and head... are all like precious food for him. And every time you touch his skin, his brain grows in leaps and bounds.

It is obvious when you stop to think about it. He has been touched and rubbed by the velvety and expanding walls of your womb holding him in place as he grows.

His skin is so sensitive that your loving touch, throughout his babyhood, will leave a 'surface memory' of feeling safe and special which will stay with him for the rest of his life.

The way we become able to give and receive love can depend upon the quality of the touch we received during our own babyhood and childhood.

> *I don't remember being picked up and cuddled and touched at all by my mum. I still feel stiff inside somehow and I don't think I'm going to be much good as a lover. I just take what I want.*
> **An eighteen-year-old boy talking about relationships**

Throughout childhood and adulthood, loving touch can speed up recovery from broken bones and torn muscles as well as ease fear, heartache and loneliness. Sensitive touch at the right moment can relax us when we are feeling tense. It can renew our flagging energy.

Loving touch is possibly the most important action and the most wonderful gift we can give to our babies, our children and to each other throughout the whole of our lives.

Hello my baby sister!

JUST WATCH!

Most parents instinctively watch their baby's face and all the little movements they make with rapt attention from the day they are born. This watching is what will help you understand what your baby is 'telling' you, every day that passes.

- Even before your baby is born he has been using his ears, his sense of taste and touch and is full already of 'this is new!' feelings. Once he is born and can begin to focus his eyes he grows fascinated by what he can see, especially smiling faces and bright colours that he has never seen before, as well as different shapes and patterns.

- You will begin to notice that everything that is happening is a new experience for him and therefore a big challenge for such a tiny person. You watch and realise how he has never before breathed air into his lungs, nor sucked and swallowed in between breaths, nor looked at different faces, shadows, colours and shapes, nor heard maybe so many different and, for him, loud and strange noises. You watch and understand how he has never seen the dazzling light from the sky or a bright electric light... nor felt his own digestion working... nor the sensation of pushing out wee or poo. You can see how he has never felt nakedness till now... nor hands, nor clothes on his skin... nor experienced the complete stillness of being laid down alone, separated from his mother.

- You notice that he is much, much more sensitive to light, sudden noise and smells than you are. Newborn babies' nervous systems are a long way from being fully developed. You see this when some little thing *startles* your newborn baby and all his muscles tighten and his arms and legs fly out, full stretch, in every direction.

- Watching closely you can see how at, only a week old, he is trying to play with you, copying your wide-open eyes, the movements of your mouth and tongue and enticing you with tiny sounds. If you copy these sounds you will see how pleased he is. If you stretch your eyes or stick your tongue out at him and he copies you, he is truly playing with you. He's picking up everything you offer him as you pick up everything he offers you.

This may not happen quite so soon if you were given medication during labour or the birth. By watching, you begin to understand his own sign language – in the movements of his face muscles, especially his mouth and eyes, and of his head, arms, legs and chest. He is trying to 'talk' to you with the whole of his body from the very beginning.

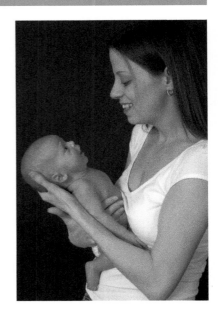

Notice especially how your baby learns to calm and settle himself to sleep. What little habits does he develop to console himself and get to sleep when he is not in your arms any longer but has been laid down somewhere?

Some babies move their head from side to side – as if they are rubbing themselves to sleep. Some flicker their eyes up. Some babies put their fists against their mouth or their cheeks or their ears. What does your baby do?

When you watch your baby closely, he will begin teaching you:

> to enjoy the moment
> to love yourself better
> to laugh
> to feel happy again after you have been sad and crying
> to trust your own instincts
> to hear your inner voice
> to see your parents in a new light and feel closer to them
> to be patient and gentle
> to slow down and calm your movements and your speaking
> to believe in yourself
> to find a rhythm – like a dance – between you both.

Is there anything you still feel worried about?

- Your own lack of sleep?
- Your baby being too hot or too cold?
- That your baby might be ill?

Some mothers can become overwhelmed by a particular, nagging worry, despite all the assurances of their midwives and health visitors. Some of these worries are entirely imaginary, some are very real. Either way, this book should help to dispel any gnawing worries that you have or help you to find ways to respond to them practically.

KANGAROO CARE AND CLOSENESS

Dads as well as mums

The best way to steady your baby after birth and in the first few weeks is through kangaroo care. Kangaroo care means laying him naked, in skin-to-skin contact, face down across your chest – and on his dad's chest – his hands and legs splayed out like a little frog and his head turned to one side for easy breathing.

Kangaroo care gives the feeling to a baby of being touched all over. Even a baby who cannot be breastfed for whatever reason will thrive with the skin-to-skin comfort of kangaroo care. This will make up for not having his face, lips and hands on your breast while you are bottle feeding him.

Kangaroo care should ideally continue for the first six to eight hours after birth or even most of the time – except when the mother is sleeping. Then for at least four to five hours each day if there is enough support there to make this easy. By then he will have a nappy on so he will not be completely naked any longer. Kangaroo care with dad – lying back in a comfy chair, on the sofa or in bed – is fabulous for babies too, as well as their dads. All you need do is unbutton your shirt! *Everyone* involved in caring for a newborn baby can get involved in kangaroo care. It's the best of the best!

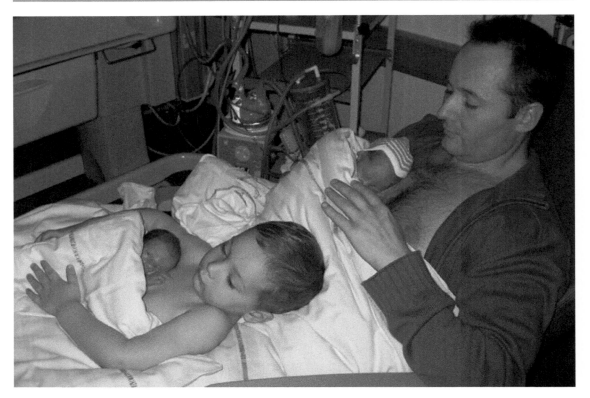

'I've got premature twin brothers! I can help too!'

Where touch begins there, also, love and humanity begins, within the first minutes following birth.
Dr Ashley Montague

Did you know?

Did you know... why skin-to-skin contact with your baby lying across your chest is the most perfect place for him to be? If he is a little too cold *your* temperature will rise two degrees to warm him. If he is a little too warm *your* temperature will fall one degree to cool him down.

Did you know... that a baby has thousands more nerve endings on every inch of his skin than he will have once he has the stretched-out space of skin of an adult?

Did you know... that it is through being gently touched on his skin that a baby's brain cells will grow well and rapidly and his spirit comes alive and thrives? He will feel happy and safe as much from your touch as from looking at your smiling face and listening to your voice.

Did you know... that even a baby with breathing difficulties immediately after birth will recover and stabilise quickly if kept in the kangaroo care position and given a touch of warmed and humidified oxygen as he lies there, rather than being taken away for intensive care in an incubator? Sometimes, of course, a baby's life will depend upon being separated from his mother in intensive care for a while, but that is another matter.

Did you know... that kangaroo care was first used in Bogota, Colombia by paediatricians who were desperate to reduce the 70% death rate in premature infants in that country? With little access to modern-day incubators they used the breast area of the mother's body with skin-to-skin, heart-to-heart contact for as many hours as possible, day and night. The miracle that resulted was that the death rate of premature babies dropped immediately to 30%. The babies who survived began to grow and thrive.

www.midwiferytoday.com/articles/kangaroocare.asp

Did you know... that kangaroo care can help all babies in these ways:

Their heart rate steadies: premature or distressed babies may lack the ability to co-ordinate their breathing and heart rates. At fussy times every baby's breathing rate increases but the heart rate doesn't necessarily keep pace, which can be distressing for them.

- ♥ Their breathing patterns become regular.
- ♥ They have more oxygen in their blood.
- ♥ They sleep for longer periods.
- ♥ They put on weight steadily.

An acute sense of smell

Within the first week, the smell of his mother becomes a baby's favourite smell – and touch is an inseparable part of that pleasure. Just look at a baby's face, sleeping in kangaroo closeness with his nose against his mother's skin, stress-free and blissful. No wonder parents begin to feel happy and proud as they become expert at holding and carrying their baby in this way.

Keeping your baby close to you

Ideally, every baby needs to be held in someone's arms or carried around in a sling as much as possible during the first nine months after birth, especially when awake. This gives him the closeness and the movement that he has been used to all his life so far. He feels completely safe and he becomes more and more interested in and understanding of what is going on around him.

Jean Leidloff in her book, *The Continuum Concept*, describes how the Yequana Indians, who live in the mountainous jungles of Venezuela, care for their babies. Those of us who do not live in mountainous jungles can still learn something about the extraordinary happiness and confidence of Yequana children and how they come to feel this way.

Even a newborn Yequana baby's day will be full of life and movement. He will be in his mother's arms or in a sling against her chest. He will sleep most of the time, but, even as he sleeps, he is learning. He is hearing the voices and laughter of everyone around him and the sounds of whatever they are doing. He soon becomes used to the bumps, the jostling and the movements that come without warning as well as the stillness that comes without warning. He is swayed and swung around and grows used to lifts and pressures on different parts of his body as he is shifted about in his mother's arms sometimes being moved from a sling on her back or front or onto her lap. All this she does for her own and her baby's comfort or to make her work easier. It becomes second nature so quickly.

Loneliness never touches a Yequana baby. Instead, his sense of safe connectedness grows steadily to his 'lover', who is his mother, and to everyone nearby. They provide a circle of welcoming arms at the ready. All the while this baby is picking up the rhythms of the day and night, changes of texture and temperature on his skin and, as Jean Leidloff describes it, 'the safe, right feeling of being held to a living body'. She also says, 'We almost certainly did exactly as they still do – until "civilisation" overtook us.'

> *I really started to think after I read The Continuum Concept. Phil had cried and fussed every day for the first two months of his life as I tried to settle him to sleep again after a feed. It was a nightmare. So I got a sling and carried him around with me almost all day instead. I showed him the ways I cleaned and cooked and tidied and every shop in the street where he lived and talked to him about what they sell. He almost never cries now. My back grew stronger so now I hardly notice the weight. The change in him is fantastic. When he gets too heavy to carry, I will have him in a baby buggy facing me so we can still talk and smile at each other.*
> **Bella**

Finding confidence and happiness

Do you feel you have any distant feelings and memories of a sad, scary or lonely babyhood and childhood yourself? If so here is your chance to change that! By lovingly nurturing your own baby now, you will be nurturing yourself and healing those old hurts.

Calmness and confidence are the two things that make it possible to calm and soothe a baby easily. Calmness and confidence usually grow out of feeling loved and valued ourselves. Feeling loved and valued is the key to gratitude and contentment.

> *I'd like to thank my dad for teaching me what a man does.*
> *I'd like to thank my mum for teaching me to give and receive love.*
> *I'd like to thank my missus for being someone for me to practise on.*
> **A father who won the Teacher of the Year awards in 2004**

When lots of mothers with new babies were asked what made them feel happy – happy enough that they really noticed it – these are some of the things they said:

> *'I feel so happy, deep down inside, when I'm holding Jodie in my arms and my husband puts his arms round us both.'*

> *'... when I watched my six-year-old lying down and kissing and snuggling our newborn, Ellie, like she was his best friend in the world. I thought: "he really will help me look after her". I felt so happy I could've cried.'*

> *'... when my baby was six weeks old and I went out to see my friends again and I realised I hadn't been forgotten and they were still there for me.'*

'... *for me, becoming a parent is an absolute joy... one of the best moments of my life. My top job is to love him like crazy. After I've showered him with affection, my next job is to feed him whenever he needs it and to calm him when he cries.*'

The next chapter introduces you to babywearing, which follows on naturally from kangaroo care.

~ CHAPTER 13 ~

Babywearing – Please Carry Me!

YOUR BABY LONGS TO BE CARRIED

Babies long to be carried. Toddlers love to be carried. They want to be close to you day and night. They reach for you, they cry for you and often it is the only thing that brings them peace in the bewildering newness of life. As you grow confident and skilled at using your sling or baby carrier, it brings you peace too. It's the best way in the world to understand and grow closer to each other as each day passes.

> *My baby has had a tough start in life and could quite easily not have made it. He has a few health problems but I know by carrying him, where he can lay his head on my heart, he feels safe and loved. The closeness we share is the greatest feeling in the world, he's with me and I'm with him and we are content.*
> **Zara**

Children have been carried in their parents' arms or in slings from the very beginning of the human story in every corner of the world.

The best book about this is *Why Babywearing Matters,* by Dr Rosie Knowles. She describes the slings and how to babywear safely. She also talks about the different cultures and the history of babywearing.

But this instinctive and essential habit somehow fell away in the developed world as industrialisation and so-called civilisation led to the widespread use of beautifully designed and costly cribs, cots, prams and buggies. For many years now, this has been considered the normal place for babies to be, day and night.

Just think for a moment!

Your baby's natural habitat is your body. You were the source of love, nourishment, safety and warmth in your womb and once he is born, he needs the same. He needs it even more so in many ways, because the outside world in which he finds himself is endlessly full of new feelings and surprises. Heat, cold, sudden bright light, different voices, different faces and sudden loud bangs are a shock to him. All this as well as learning to suck and swallow and fit that in with breathing steadily.

He will manage it all beautifully if he is still closely connected to you by being in your arms or in a sling. But it will be much harder for him and he will more often and more quickly grow distressed if he is put down in a 'container', alone and lonely for any longish period of time – unless he is sleeping peacefully.

If you live in a crowded, noisy city, which more and more parents find themselves doing these days, it could be even more important to wear your baby.

One of the best ways of providing this sense of love and security to your baby has always been to carry him in your arms, right from birth and also to be able to pass him from one pair of loving arms to the next. This support is now often missing if members of a family live far apart and close friends are at work.

If you find yourself in this situation – it needs courage to do this – could you watch out for any warm, smiling faces amongst the women who live nearby and somehow introduce yourself, spend time with them, make friends with them and talk to them often enough to know that they are calm and sensible with babies and children and that you trust them? Could you ask one or two of them to help you sometimes by being 'stand-in' arms to hold your baby (like a 'nan' or 'auntie') when you need a break?

Babies and children who grow up in close communities where they are deeply loved, respected and shared around amongst several adults have a huge advantage. They feel welcomed, safe and valued. They know they belong. Their world expands and they learn about love from the very first day of their lives.

But carrying your newborn baby in your arms or having him on your lap is hard work if there is no one else there every day to help you in the early weeks. It means you can't easily do anything else at all!

THE BEST SOLUTION IS BABYWEARING

The best-of-all alternative to baby carrying is 'babywearing' – taking us back to our ancestors – using a sling or carrier and carrying your newborn against your chest, able to feel your heartbeat, smell your skin, hear your voice and every breath you take, also to feel every movement you make, just as it was in the womb. Your hands are free and your baby is close enough to kiss. You can see each other's face. Your baby is close enough to see your smile. This is brilliant!

> *Babies that are carried like this tend to suckle more which in turn helps to maintain their mothers' milk supply, just as needed, day by day.*
> **Dr Sears**

These slings and baby carriers, when used safely, make your life much easier as well as providing the close contact that your baby needs and will thrive on. Being that close also allows your baby to see and sense what is going on around him and to feel part of life more quickly and fully. This does much to help his rapidly developing brain.

There are many different designs for you to try out and discover what is best for you. There is practical help at hand to make sure you choose the carrier that suits you and your baby and develop the skills and confidence to make it work beautifully for you. It needs familiarity and practice – like learning to ride a bike.

Rhythm and movement

When there is rhythm in your voice, in your movements and in music and singing around your baby it has a powerful effect on his brain development, sense of belonging and happiness.

When your baby spends enough time each day close against your living body, his breathing rate, his heart rate and his temperature control will settle and steady. You will be hands free and movement free. There will be an increase of oxytocin (the love hormone) in your body.

> 'I love being able to go anywhere, do almost anything, and still keep my baby close to me. Bus journeys are a breeze, car boots are pram free!'
>
> 'A stretchy sling helped me build a bond with my difficult baby who would not be put down. And it helped me through postnatal depression.'

But babies need more than just your closeness and touch. Rocking, swaying or swinging a fussing or crying baby will help to bring peace quickly. Imagine what it must have been like for him during the last month or two of your pregnancy: dark, warm, contained within soft flexible walls, rhythmic movement, the muffled sound of your heart beating, your blood pulsing, your regular breathing and the quiet tones of your voice. His birth was a dramatic ejection into space, brightness, loud noises, sudden stillness and rapid movement. No wonder your baby needs to be picked up and held close for hours on end and sleeps easily when he is cuddled on your chest.

Dr Rosie Knowles is a mum and a doctor (GP). She set up and runs the Sheffield Sling Surgery, a consultancy and sling library service. www.sheffieldslingsurgery.co.uk

Through Rosie you will receive outstanding advice and encouragement about how to get started with a sling. Through the Sheffield Sling Surgery website, under Education, you can see excellent videos on the use of all the different kinds of slings and carriers.

www.babyslingsafety.co.uk gives you the T.I.C.K.S Rule for Safe Babywearing, with illustrations.

There are also three simple, essential rules for you to memorise from Babywearing International:

A – Airway: Remember how heavy your baby's head is in relation to the rest of his body. Make sure his airway stays open by ensuring that his chin is off his chest and make sure that air is circulating round his face, two fingers width between his chin and his chest.

B – Body position: Make sure that your baby sling/carrier holds your baby with his upper body against your chest to give support to his neck. And that it is tight enough to prevent him slipping down and rolling into a ball like a hedgehog. He will *feel* safe and *be* safe if he is carried with his knees higher than his bum and his weight borne by his thighs and bottom.

C – Comfort: The sling/carrier you choose must be comfortable for you as well as your baby. If you do not feel comfortable and confident you need help from your local babywearing adviser.

Dr William Sears, an American paediatrician, has been describing the benefits and encouraging babywearing since the 1980s. To find out more, see:

www.askdrsears.com/?s=Babywearing

https://slingpages.slinginglondon.co.uk/

A simple, one-stop website to help you find your local sling resources quickly and easily in the UK/Eire.

www.babywearinginternational.org encourages babywearing as an accepted and universal practice.

If, for any reason, it would be impossible for you to carry your baby, think about the importance of using a buggy or pram with your baby facing you so that he can see your smile and you can 'talk' to each other. Otherwise, it's nothing but the legs of strangers, pavements or tree trunks!

~ CHAPTER 14 ~

Valuable Baby-Calming Skills For New Parents

These skills can make a big difference to parents trying to understand and look after their crying baby. Each will need practice and perseverance until they become easy habits for you.

'TALKING' TO YOUR NEWBORN BABY

Many remarkable people, especially T. Berry Brazelton in America (www.brazeltontouchpoints.org), Joanna Hawthorne at the Brazelton Centre for Family Research in Cambridge, UK (www.brazelton.co.uk) and Vivien Sabel (www.viviensabel.com) with her 'Blossom Method' have been working on the same research and helping parents to understand how intelligent and capable their babies are even moments after their birth. These people show us so carefully and well how to read the clues our babies are giving us – in their face, their eyes and with their hands – and how to respond to these clues so that an enchanting communication can start to develop between you from the first few days of your baby's life.

As soon as your baby has begun to recover from the never-felt-before pressures and exhaustion of being born and learning to breathe, he will lock onto you with his eyes and try to see your face. Most often this will happen in the first few minutes when he is still full of adrenaline. Within a week you will be able to notice his different expressions, the tiny movements of his lips, tongue, mouth and face. Also the movements of his head, hands, arms and legs. The more you can 'listen with your eyes' the more quickly you will pick up the different messages he is trying again and again to tell you without being able to speak a word.

WATCH, MIRROR AND RESPOND

♥ If you can watch closely and carefully enough you will be able to see exactly what he is doing with the muscles of his face, especially with his lips and his tongue – as well as other movements he is making with any part of his body. Then wait for him to do the same again.

♥ With your face close enough for him to see you, copy exactly what you see him doing, as far as you are able. If he responds by making the same pattern of movements again, a simple, gentle conversation between you both has begun! Then, if you keep watching his face closely enough, whenever he is alert and looking at you, you will notice which patterns of movement he repeats when he knows you are watching. He is trying to communicate with you! And you will begin to understand what he means with each movement. For example, an O-shaped mouth, or tongue moving in and out can mean 'I'm hungry. Please feed me.' Dreamy eyes with tongue lolling on the bottom lip can mean 'I'm full to bursting with milk and air, please burp me.' Every baby is different and each will try to tell you things in different ways. You need to watch and watch and keep guessing until you recognise his 'sign language'.

♥ If you always mirror back to him straightaway his expressions and movements and tiny sounds, *before* you feed him, burp him, cuddle him or change his nappy, a wonderful understanding between you will soon grow, and you won't be asking yourself 'What's he crying for now?' He won't need to cry because you've answered his needs already. The more you understand each other through this skill, the more peaceful and contented those early weeks will be for you both.

♥   Always say out loud, in just a few words, what you think he is telling you: 'You need a feed'; 'Time for a nappy change'; 'You are tired'. With a little pause to watch his response. He loves your familiar voice and he's so intelligent that he will soon be fitting the signing and the spoken word together like a jigsaw puzzle.

♥   When this communication between you is firmly in place, you can introduce new signs yourself for your baby to pick up from you. A closed hand touching your mouth and shut eyes, meaning 'time to sleep'. Wide open eyes and big smile, 'I'm feeling happy, I love you!' The understanding and loving communication between you both will just keep growing.

THE THUMPING HEEL SWAY

This mother-and-baby calming skill was taught to me by an Ananda Marga nun working in a Sunrise School in Holland and helping mothers with their crying babies. The Thumping Heel Sway is such a useful skill that it is also described in another Right from the Start book: *Sound Sleep: Calming and Helping Your Baby or Child to Sleep.*

It is a skill being used by parents and carers all over the world.

This is how to do it:

1.   Stand with your feet planted firmly and comfortably apart, just wider than your hips.

2.   Hold your baby upright against your left shoulder at whatever level feels easy for you. If your shoulder is very bony or your baby is hiccoughy or sickuppy, lay a pad over your shoulder first. Left is best because he can feel your heartbeat more strongly that side.

3.   Have one hand under his buttocks like an egg in an eggcup and your other hand, with fingers spread, across his shoulders (or across his head and shoulders if he is still tiny and wobbly).

4.   Now, keeping the soles of your feet on the same spot, begin to sway your body slowly and rhythmically from left to right to left again with stiff, straight legs. Lift each heel in turn up off the ground, high enough to be able to thump it down again firmly with each body swing.

This sends a heart-beat-like tremor through your body into your baby. The slow, steady thump... thump... thump of your heels bumping on the ground is mesmerising and comforting for both of you. The graceful, rhythmic, swaying movement is less tiring for you than walking anxiously up and down or sitting jiggling your baby in all sorts of different positions to try to stop the crying.

Practise this until it becomes an easy and automatic movement. You can also hold him so his head is pressing gently against your cheek and hum to him quietly as you sway and thump.

Unless he is crying from hunger, the Thumping Heel Sway will calm him within two minutes. Have a bet with yourself!

The reason it works so well is that it makes you feel more confident and peaceful yourself and your baby can smell you and feel your heartbeat – exaggerated by the thump of your heels. The steady, even rhythm is calming because it feels to your baby a bit like being back in the womb as you were walking along.

Unlike a lamb or a foal, staggering around on wobbly legs within minutes of being born and starting to run around a day later, our babies are totally helpless and vulnerable for the first three months of life. They are actually born three months too early out of necessity. The size of the human brain is so great that they have to be born early for the skull to be able to pass through the birth canal. This is why these particular baby-calming skills are so valuable to learn for those first few months.

CALMING YOUR SCREAMING BABY

> *One day, when my Billy started crying and it began to build up into screaming my mum said to me 'try kissing him before the crying gets going. It's easier to stop the crying starting up than to stop the screaming ten minutes later, when the crying has taken on a life of its own!'*
> **Ju**

An internationally well-known paediatrician and child development specialist called Dr Harvey Karp has developed a way of turning off a baby's screams like switching off a light.

This *switch* is not magic or a miracle, it is a reflex that all babies are born with. Babies are run by reflexes. These built-in abilities ensure that they can breathe, cry, suck and swallow from the first moment of birth. Babies are also born with a *calming reflex* like a shut-off switch for infant crying.

Reflexes are very reliable, but very particular. If anyone hits your knee in exactly the right place, your foot jerks out. It will work every time. But, if it is done too softly or in the wrong place, absolutely nothing happens.

Unlike a hit on the knee, there are five specific steps which turn on a baby's calming reflex.

Mothers all over the world know instinctively that, to calm their baby, they need to imitate the sensations of being in the womb. Mothers shush their baby with a loud whooshy sound and also rock and jiggle their baby in their arms when they start to cry.

Dr Harvey Karp teaches mothers how to mimic even more perfectly a baby's sensations in the womb. He describes, and also demonstrates in his DVD, *The Happiest Baby on the Block*, the five steps (the '5 S's', he calls them) which switch on a baby's calming reflex:

1. Swaddling your baby: By the last three months, your baby has been tightly packaged in the womb with almost no room left to move and comforting walls touching him on all sides. There are many different kinds of special swaddling cloths and blankets to mimic this feeling of tight safety during the first three months after birth. They have clear instructions about their use which must be followed carefully.

2. Side-stomach: Newborn babies are easier to calm when they are lying on their side or stomach because it imitates more closely the way they lay in the womb. Hold your swaddled baby, tummy down, on your arm, with his head cradled in your hand, facing outwards. Practise holding him in exactly this position, lying on his stomach along your arm and tipped over onto his left side – but not tipped so far over that your mouth cannot reach his ear. Hold him in this position firmly and as calmly as you can, however loudly he is still screaming.

3. Shushing: Put your lips near your baby's ear and start making a long, loud shushing sound. Start quietly, then build up the shushing until it is almost as loud as your baby is crying so he can hear you! Keep it going without a pause, except to take a quick breath between each shush! Sushhhhhhhhhh... Sushhhhhhhhhh... Sushhhhhhhhhh. Because this copies the loud swishing sounds he heard in the womb (like a vacuum cleaner running!), it says to him 'Don't worry. Everything is fine.' Fade out your shushing and move your mouth further away from his ear as he becomes calm.

It can also help if you hold your hand gently flat on his tummy – just a light touch at the same time as you shush him.

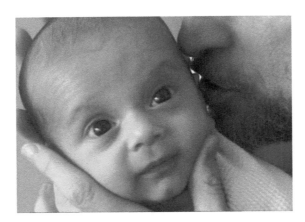

Keep practising these first three steps till they become so familiar that you hardly have to think. You may have already switched on his calming reflex and will not need to follow with steps 4 and 5. You will know at once because the look in his eyes will be one of surprise and pleasure.

4. **S**winging: A rhythmic, hypnotising movement is nourishing for all of us, whatever age we are. The swinging movements that your baby experienced in the womb when you walked around or climbed up stairs, or biked, or danced or swam also help to activate this calming reflex.

     This is one way to do it. Lay your baby along your legs, facing you, with your arms on either side of him and your hands on your knees, cradling his head. Keep your knees together and, using a very small movement, swing from side-to-side. Remember to be gentle, never jerky or rough in any way.

     By watching his face and the little wobble of his head in your hands, you will learn to judge which is the speed that soothes him. Slow down the movement as he grows peaceful.

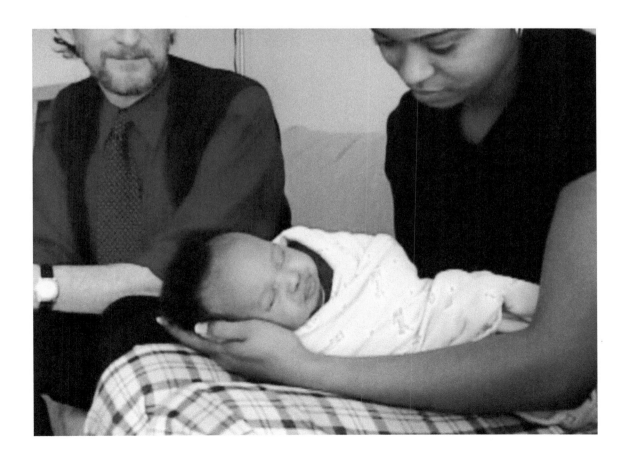

5. **S**ucking: Sucking means much more to a baby than a mouthful of milk. The action of sucking releases endorphins from your baby's brain and these help to calm him. This is why babies often need to suck, even when they are not necessarily still hungry. This is why they sometimes need urgently to suck their fists, your finger or a dummy to comfort and calm themselves. It helps to make sure that one of them is always within easy reach. If your baby does not at first find it easy to hold a dummy in his mouth and suck – instead of pushing it into his mouth, lightly tap it down onto his bottom lip to start the sucking reflex.

When my baby started crying in the supermarket, of course I couldn't easily stop and do the whole 5 S's there and then! But I did lift Yanec up, wrap him snugly, held him in the facing down and out position along my arm and did a bit of shushing and swinging. I asked the person behind me at the checkout to unload my trolley for me. Most people in public places are glad to do anything to quieten the screams! It worked so quickly and I stopped feeling all tensed up and desperate to get home.
Marijke

To find out more, see: www.happiestbaby.com

Music for Dreaming has been created by Cherie A. Ross especially for babies and their parents so they may feel comforted and nurtured. The lullabies, played by the Melbourne Symphony Orchestra as one continuous piece, mimic the womb and heartbeat sounds your baby heard in the last months before birth. Gentle and harmonic music can have a profoundly calming and healing effect on us all. Flute, strings and harp are the main instruments.

> *I played Music for Dreaming while I was pregnant and at the hospital during labour. It is still doing wonders, better than any dummy for settling. The music signals quiet time or sleep times. Hayden was born to it, now he's growing with it.*
> **Theresa Thomas in Australia**

www.musicfordreaming.com

The Silent Path, a CD by Robert Haig Coxon, offers you a magical musical journey, bringing you to a deep state of relaxation, meditation and peace. You can listen to *The Silent Path* on YouTube:

www.youtube.com/watch?v=O7sf8T8G-go

CHAPTER 15

Is your baby's crying still a big worry?

For many parents the most difficult thing at first is how to work out what is wrong and then discover what helps to calm their crying or screaming baby.

You may be feeling too tired to think! Your ears can be particularly sensitive to the individual pitch of your baby's crying, so that it upsets you a lot to listen to it. A lot of crying can lead to disturbed nights and a serious shortage of sleep. This can numb your brain.

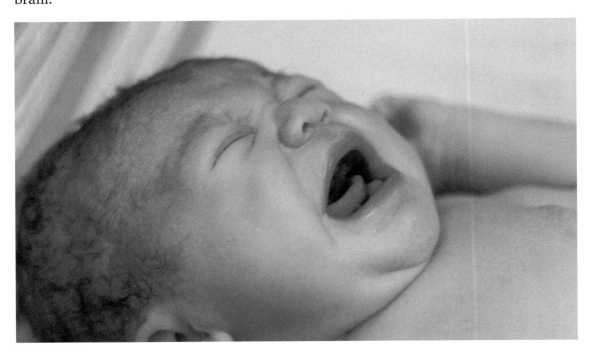

I used to get in such a panic whenever my baby woke up and cried loudly. I could feel it like a pain in my throat and in my tummy.
Sarah

WHY DOES MY BABY CRY SO MUCH?

Crying is the only language a baby has and he will begin to cry the moment he begins to need you for food or comfort. You will soon learn the different reasons for your baby's crying by the sound of it, the intensity of it and when it happens. The discomfort that starts your baby off crying could be physical or could be a sudden noise or jolt, or just general tension.

Obvious physical causes are hunger, sore bottom and nappy needs changing, sun or a bright light in his eyes, tummy ache from trapped wind or colic resulting from something in your milk.

> *I had to stop drinking coffee, tea and Coke because the stimulants went straight to my baby and upset him.*
> **Pat**

There are also tensions in some babies which are more difficult to pin down. A long and overwhelming or painful birth sometimes causes what is called birth trauma in a newborn baby. A traumatised baby may be unbelievably quiet and immobile for the first few days after birth, but then begin to cry and cry, sometimes it seems almost non-stop, to get rid of some of the pain and fear he has been through. This may continue for several weeks – even a few months – and can be desperately worrying and exhausting, for mothers in particular, especially if they can't understand the reason for the crying.

> *My midwife was wonderful. She explained what the problem might be so clearly. She helped me sort out my day so that I could make sure I could walk around carrying my baby in my arms or in a sling on my chest whenever the crying started. She helped me to find the holding position in my arms that helped best to soothe him.*
> **Zinzi**
>
> *Our baby daughter never seemed to stop crying for three months after the birth. We both got frantic. Carrying her round all the time, cuddling her and talking to her did help a bit but it was only when we were advised to take her to see a cranial osteopath that the tension really left her and she became peaceful and happy. He somehow applied such gentle pressure to the right spots around her head, neck and spine that the tension left in her from the birth seemed to be released in just a few moments.*
> **Fred**

SCREAMING FITS

There's nothing more worrying and distressing for parents than the experience of holding a screaming baby in their arms and being unable to comfort him and stop the horror going on and on. The sound in your ears is so painful it freezes you. The sight of his little face, purple with distress, his wide-open mouth and quivering tongue, the build-up of heat, his rapid breathing and heaving ribs soon become agonising – especially if you are alone together. Sometimes the pitch of a baby's cry can seem as awful as having a dentist drill in your own mouth. If it feels that awful for you get some earplugs and concentrate on keeping moving, slowly and rhythmically with him in your arms.

Here are some suggestions to help you discover what will help you:

- ♥ Do anything you can that will calm you enough to help you sit quietly for a moment and be able to think. Read again 'Putting yourself first' in Chapter 3.
- ♥ Meanwhile, keep holding him in your arms or in a sling and get walking whenever you have the energy.
- ♥ Try to get him sucking if he will, or stroke his top lip if he's too distressed to suck. Try this, even as you walk about. Sometimes the combination of the two does the trick.
- ♥ See if taking your baby outside and walking around in the fresh air will soothe him.

♥ What you are eating? Is there something that is upsetting his digestion and causing sudden pain? It could be the dairy products, acid fruits or stimulants like coffee, Coke, tea and curry that you're eating or drinking. Could you cut them out, one at a time, and see if that helps over the next few days?

♥ Was there a sudden loud noise that might have shocked him or has he been hearing loud music or shouting?

♥ What other calming skills could you try? How about the Thumping Heel Sway in Chapter 14?

♥ Ask your midwife or health visitor for advice. Your baby's screaming in the early weeks may be actually helping your baby. It can contract and stretch the muscles round his face and neck strongly enough to help the moulding of his skull after the pressures of birth return to normal again. But sometimes neither sucking nor screaming can complete this recovery and he may need help from a cranial osteopath (see the resources list).

Remember that it might take up to three weeks of steady perseverance with some of these suggestions to bring about a lasting change. Screaming can become a habit in a baby, like everything else, and habits can't be changed in a couple of days.

NEVER, NEVER, EVER SMACK OR SHAKE YOUR BABY

Decide now that however tired you are, however alone and desperate you feel, however angry you feel towards your baby for crying and screaming you will *never, ever* – in your rage and misery – smack him, shake him or throw him down. Can you sense the panic and anger rising up in you in time, *before* you become overwhelmed by it? Could you make yourself lay your baby down gently in a safe place and leave him there to cry while you look after yourself?

Now, leave him for ten minutes while you: drink some water... rub the back of your neck... beat up a cushion... take some deep breaths outside, if possible. Next, telephone a friend, your health visitor or a neighbour with children who has smiled at you. Ask for help urgently from someone – anyone you know even a little but trust – to go walkabout with your baby out of sight and out of earshot, even for twenty minutes. Best of all if they can then stay a little longer with you both, to talk and be a comfort.

When your baby is back in your arms, whether quieter or still crying, lie down and suckle him to calm you both. If he's still too churned up, walk about with him slowly and rhythmically and talk to him quietly. Tell him how unhappy you feel when he cries. Tell him you will *never* hurt him. Tell him you wish you understood why he feels so distressed. Guess the answers to your questions and tell him – just as if he could understand every word you say. He soon will! And remember to tell him you love him.

However, if crying is a continuing worry for you, there is a Right from the Start 'sister' book to this one: *Sound Sleep: Calming and Helping Your Baby or Child to Sleep*. Chapter 2, Understanding a New Baby's Crying, Chapter 3, When Crying Becomes Screaming, and Chapter 4, How to Cope, will give you even more practical support and ideas.

We had no idea that it would be that difficult and she'd cry day after day. We got desperate. You come home from hospital with a sweet baby. They never really tell you how intense it all is until you live it.
Phoebe

My baby, after a long birth, never seemed to stop crying. When he was two weeks old, I started doing the 'Thumping Heel Sway' with him after every feed and whenever he started screaming. A week later, I realised that it was working a treat. He would stop crying within two minutes every time. The rhythm of it became so automatic it relaxed me too.
Selma

More than anything else you do for your baby, it will be the energy of your loving spirit, springing from your soul that will turn difficulties into joy.

~ CHAPTER 16 ~

Your Spirit and your Soul

The energy in your body does not only come from the sun that shines on you, the food you eat, the water you drink, the air you breathe, the exercise you take and the healing and recovery that comes from your sleeping. There are other sources too.

ELECTROMAGNETIC ENERGY

There is an electromagnetic energy in you, like invisible 'vibrations' running through you. These vibrations are inaudible. You cannot hear them. But you can sense them in subtle ways when something you see – perhaps a smile, a bird, a place you love or something said to you which touches your heart – makes you feel suddenly sensitive and alert, or full of empathy and understanding, or deeply loved or loving.

This vibrational energy runs up and down your spine and around your body from your toes and fingers to the top of your head. It moves up and then down from the lowest, physical energy levels up to the highest spiritual energy levels – and then down again. The highest frequencies (vibrations) of this energy are concentrated around your heart, your throat and the fore-part of your brain – the prefrontal cortex.

The electromagnetic energy running from north to south and through and around the earth matches exactly the electromagnetic energy running through and around each one of us. Recent discoveries show that we replenish our own electromagnetic energy directly from the earth whenever we are in direct touch with the ground, sitting, lying or walking barefoot on grass or sand or rock. We need to connect with earth energies all our lives to be healthy and feel good.

www.groundology.co.uk/videos?show=clint-ober-earthing-research

THE ENERGY OF LOVE

The highest, pulsing vibrations in our hearts and our heads are the spiritual energy flowing in us. They have the greatest impact on our personality, on our ability to forgive each other, think and act selflessly, treat each other with love and respect, and comfort each other during sad or hard times.

The spiritual energy of love in each of us is a free-wheeling energy. It is sometimes called the 'higher self'. Sometimes it is called the 'third eye'. Often this spiritual, creative energy is just called 'love'. Many people name it 'God' or 'Allah' or the Divine (or one of over a hundred other names used for 'God' in different parts of the world) or they find their own word to describe it.

This energy of love is the way forward to growing in confidence and wisdom. This spiritual energy inside each of us, spreading to our families and neighbours, is the only way that peace can come to our communities and reach across the world.

> *As we selflessly love, care for, treasure and teach our babies and children, so will they, in turn, grow in spirit and in loving energy and help to make the world a better place.*
> **Helen Wilson**

YOUR SPIRIT IS THE ENERGY OF YOUR SOUL

The soul is the name that is often given to the source of this indestructible and loving energy in each one of us. What we call our soul is part of us from the moment our body begins to grow in the womb until the end of our life, and maybe, who knows, on and on until the end of time. It is the spiritual energy from our soul that leads us to search for, and maybe choose, one particular religious faith or another to support what we feel and hunger for, and long to understand more fully. This searching may go on throughout our life as we try to make sense of the feelings in our heart and the thoughts in our head, and to discover who we are and the purpose in our life. When we give birth to a child, this search can intensify and perhaps change us forever.

Young children

Young children are very sensitive to this bright and shining vibration inside them because of their vulnerability and innocence. They are born with a feeling of belonging to the whole world – being connected to everything they see and touch and smell and hear. They can become our teachers when we pay enough attention to them and watch and listen to them carefully. Through them we can recover what we may have lost through the worrying and hurrying of adult life.

> *Only our heart-mind communication makes it possible to become aware of the loving, spiritual energy in ourselves, in each other and in the whole of creation. Myths and power-structured religions can take us away from the natural awareness of this loving, spiritual energy everywhere.*
> **Meister Eckhart**

Our creative imagination and intuition lie mainly in the right side of our brain working closely with our pre-frontal cortex (the fore-brain). It is the ponderings between these parts of our brain, working with the love energy from our heart, which give us the ability to grow wise, make good decisions and build loving and lasting relationships. We feel part of the wholeness and goodness of life.

When a really big thing happens to us like giving birth or a really sudden, unexpected twist in life such as the death of someone close, a brain shift or spirit shift will happen in us. This inner shift may lead us to start searching, in a deeper way, for a new path or purpose in our lives.

It is the intelligence in our heart that feeds our best intuition into our mind. It is now well researched that the intensity of the electromagnetic vibrations from our heart is much more powerful than the electromagnetic vibrations from our brain. Our loving, spiritual energy is concentrated in our heart.

As we 'think with our heart' so we are. Children know this from babyhood. It's only eighteen inches from head to heart. Instant connection and communication to help us grow in wisdom and in devotion and care of each other.

When heart to brain connection is not there

> *I can never forget talking to a lone mum with four young children in Hackney, London. Unloved and neglected throughout her own childhood she burst out to me:*
> *'My life's 'ell. Every day. Kids fightin' and me shoutin' at 'em an' hittin' 'm wiv whatever I'm holdin'. The mess everywhere an' the dump we lives in. Neighbours from hell too. Don't come near us!'*

What we call 'Hell' is not a place. Hell is the here-and-now of what we are feeling and thinking and the way we are behaving to each other – cursing and shouting, lashing out and furious, unresolved arguments. It can be worrying, complaining and filling with anger and hatred. Hell can be getting stuck in grief or shackled by fear. Hell can also be the loneliness of just existing and choosing not to go further. It can be a shutting away of hope and courage.

If we frequently come to feel, think and behave in hellish ways, we forget all about the intelligence and loving power of our heart and mind. This power helps us to love and accept ourselves just as we are now, as we cope as best we can with our lives. It helps us, however rich or poor we are, to discover ways to bring love, fun and celebration into our own and our children's lives.

Loving is like a special kind of active prayer

> *Prayer is the quality of loving. Praying is no prayer unless it has compassion and empathy and love and a deep sense of genuine caring for whoever we are praying for. Love is the only key able to unlock any door.*
> **Larry Dossey, MD, Humana Medical City,**
> **Dallas and National Institute of Health**

Many people find a sense of their own soul by listening to music they love or walking or sitting quietly on their own in green and beautiful places.

> *There is a soul force in the universe which, if we allow it, will flow through us and produce miraculous results.*
> **Mahatma Gandhi**

Everyone has faith in something or someone, even if it is just faith in a close friend or the arrival of summer or the postman. Some people go a step further and recognise the spiritual energy in their own lives and in the lives of some of those around them as sudden surges of peace and joy without any seeming cause. Some have faith in a particular spiritual leader or religious faith to give them a way of loving and living, which also nourishes their spirit – Christ or great prophets and teachers like Buddha, Mohammed, Gandhi, Sri Aurobindo, Khalil Gibran, Martin Luther King, Mother Teresa and many others over the centuries.

The purest, most peaceful and courageous part of you is your spirit. Your spirit is the brimming energy of your soul. Your soul is the everlasting and ever-present source of the 'goodness' or 'Godness' in you. Nothing can destroy it. It is always there, in you and in your baby, to see you safely through times of difficulty, distress or despair and to fill you with joy at unexpected moments.

What will come next?

The next Right from the Start books for new parents will be:

- *Best Beginnings: the Amazing Development of Your Baby During the First Nine Months.*
- *Best Beginnings: the First Three Years. A Very Special Time.*

These are a continuation of *Best Beginnings for Your Baby and You.*

You can keep up-to-date via our website: www.right-from-the-start.org

Provision of greater emotional and spiritual support, especially for mothers, has become critical now that so many new parents have minimal face-to-face time with their midwives and health visitors, caused by the present shortfall of these professionals. The widespread scatter of extended family members, particularly grandparents, is another factor in the lack of day-by-day support.

These three central books for expectant and new parents have also been written to provide understnding and information about the emotional and spiritual needs of parents and their babies for midwives, health visitors and social workers in training.

They are also for use by sixth formers attending parenting courses in school or college.

Protecting your baby's health in the womb

Fresh, organic fruit and vegetables – especially green, leafy vegetables, eaten on a daily basis – are *absolutely essential* for expectant mothers!

A baby in the womb, minute-by-minute and second-by-second, is growing every part of his body at full tilt, starting with just a bunch of cells looking like a tiny, newly formed blackberry. Then, full speed ahead, come the heart, brain, eyes, ears, nose, mouth, lungs, kidneys, liver, pancreas, bones and tendons, arms and legs, fingers and toes.

A baby can only grow successfully, beautifully and completely if all the essential nutrients are available and reach him continuously through the umbilical cord, without any 'slow-downs' or gaps. Slow-downs and gaps are the instant and direct result of a mother eating a poor diet or drinking alcohol, taking drugs or smoking.

The effect of an expectant mother's ongoing stress and eating sugary, processed foods can be disastrous for her unborn child and that child's adult health in the future.

It is only in the last few decades – since the 1960s – that we have been eating ever larger amounts of processed and adulterated foods, almost all of them containing toxic additives of one kind or another – preservatives, taste enhancers, colouring. Also, much of the meat and poultry we eat from today's supermarkets have been fed growth enhancers or antibiotics to protect them from the rapid spread of disease in crowded, indoor living conditions. Remnants of these are then absorbed, causing subtle disruptions to the health of adults and threatening the infinitely delicate and non-stop development of a baby in the womb.

Major research projects in recent years – mainly in the USA – show how clear and powerful the relationship is between a mother's diet, if lacking in vital nutrients and containing toxins, and the present and growing epidemic of low birth weight and preterm babies, also, autism, Down's syndrome, ADHD, childhood obesity and childhood diabetes. For example, in the USA during the last sixty years, autism has risen from one child in 10,000 to one child in 166. This link to an article by Donna Gates gives you valuable information, especially about how a mother's nutrition and lifestyle can have a positive impact on her child's immune system upon which his future health will depend:

https://bodyecology.com/articles/womanneedstoknowhaveababy.php

It's not just about nutrition...

Trying to bear alone and recover from long-lasting stress or a big grief, without support and comfort, will have an equally harmful effect on the steady, healthy development of your unborn baby. What a mother feels, hour by hour and day by day, so does her baby absorb and carry with him throughout the pregnancy and out into the world when he is born. (See 'Ways to help yourself' in Chapter 3: What Help and Encouragement Do *You* Need?)

> *Your baby can sense whether you are happy or sad, agitated or calm. In essence, your baby feels what you feel. Your baby eats what you eat.*
> **Donna Gates**

Obesity and Childbirth

Being seriously overweight can be a nightmare, especially for women who become pregnant and for their babies. It is a nightmare because it stops you feeling good about yourself. You don't feel well or energetic. You worry about your looks, your double chins, your swollen legs, your clothes and whether there will be room for your bum on the bus and whether it will be safe to sit on someone else's chair in case it breaks. It is no joking matter and all the harder to cope with because it need not have happened in the first place. Many women who become obese feel, too, that they have reached a point of no return and can't even think how they might reverse their weight gain habit, let alone find the strength and the help they will need to achieve a big weight loss and stay steady.

These six women describe what obesity feels like for them:

'It's like you can't escape. There are fast food outlets, two-for-one offers in supermarkets and huge, bright, blow-up adverts for food and drink whichever way you look. There is ready-made food under your nose all the time, unless you are in the middle of a field or up a hill, right away from any shops.'

'I eat biscuits or crisps or chocolates or have a Coke whenever I need to wind down.'

'You want to eat something as soon as you feel a bit bored or lonely. Sometimes you want to eat as soon as you sit down.'

'Eating fatty food fills me up and calms me down. It makes me feel sleepy and comfortable.'

'I think I started eating every hour or two to comfort myself. It's now got to be a habit I can't break.'

'I know I eat too much, too often and mostly the wrong food and drink, and hardly take any exercise. But I don't know how to start changing the way I live.'

I love eating and now there doesn't seem much else to do. I'm too fat to go out much and I know I must be horrible to look at. I feel a failure and ashamed, even when I see other very fat people in the street, too. I try hard not to show how I feel. I try to keep smiling when I'm in public places.'

Seriously overweight adults almost invariably share their lifestyle with their children, so the whole family may soon show signs of becoming overweight too.

The more food that is eaten at one sitting, the bigger the stomach is stretched to hold it... and the quicker the feeling of hunger returns again, even after two hours. It's easy to test this out yourself and notice when you feel empty again.

USEFUL KNOWLEDGE AND INFORMATION

Dr David Servan-Schreiber is the founder of the Center for Integrative Medicine at the University of Pittsburgh Medical Centre. Also a psychiatrist, Dr David had developed a brain tumour himself which conventional treatment had failed to prevent re-occurring. He recognised that only extensive knowledge about protective, anti-cancer foods might save his life. In 2008 he presented his findings simply and clearly in a book called *Anti-cancer: a New Way of Life.*

As he became more deeply involved in researching cancer-causing foods and pollutants, he stumbled upon the main reason why obesity has become an ever-spreading plague in many industrialised countries. He also discovered the reasons why the courage and determination of individual people to prevent or reverse their own massive weight gain so often ends in failure and a lifetime of ill health.

Talking about obesity in his book, he confirms that people eat when they are not hungry because they are feeling anxious or angry or because their day is empty of interest. He then goes on to describe how much of the food which people eat regularly is food which has been tampered with in one very specific way or another and had its 'character' changed. He discovered that the changes in the character of particular foods, through this tampering, are the chief cause of excessive and continuous weight gain, despite every effort to prevent it. Food that has been tampered with can change the way your brain works. This means that sometimes the messages from your brain to your body about the need to store fat can go seriously awry. This is where research about obesity is now being concentrated.

A few people have a genetic effect – a defective gene which drives them to eat high-fat food as if their brain is telling them they are starving. The same defect prevents them burning the fat that is piling on.

Essential fatty acids

The essential fatty acids are called omega-3 and omega-6. We get these special fats through the food we eat. We cannot do without them. The crux of the matter is that the right balance between the omega-3 and omega-6 in our bodies is crucial to all our body functions. Our bodies need twice as much omega-3 as omega-6, more or less in the ratio of 2 to 1. If what we eat gives us much more omega-6 than omega-3, the proper balance is lost, and omega-6 will be in control of our body's functions. Amongst other health problems, this imbalance will cause our bodies to store fat continuously. There will also be rigidity in our cells and coagulation and inflammation which can prevent weight loss, however hard we try to achieve it.

There is another fatty acid called omega-9. It is mainly protective and not so essential as 3 and 6.

How did things go wrong?

Since the 1940s, because of commercial interests and growing city populations, the food industry has forced big changes to be made to farming methods and ways of preserving food. These have been the two major changes:

1. First, discovering how to turn liquid vegetable oils into solid fat to become spreadable margarine and to have a far longer shelf life than newly pressed oil. It can then be used in many other foods on the supermarket shelves such as cakes, biscuits, pizza, crisps and many ready-made meals, so they do not become stale or go rancid. Some can sit on the shelf for months.

   These oils, through the ways in which they are treated in order to become solid, become in part 'transfats', 'saturated fats' or 'hydrogenated fats'. These are known to be harmful. Further harm comes from the loss of the right omega-3 to omega-6 ratio of 1 to 1 or at most 2 to 1. Eating foods containing these 'concocted' fats may give us an imbalance of 1 to 15 or worse, so that many people have far too little omega-3 in their bodies and far too much omega-6, and then they begin steadily to put on weight.

2. In just the same way, slowly but surely, ever since the Second World War, there has been a big change of 'character' in the meat, poultry and eggs we eat and the milk we drink because of new farming methods and the manufacture and over-use of concentrated and less natural animal feeds.

What has gone wrong?

The main cause of our troubles is the changes in animal care. Beef and dairy cattle and pigs, as well as chickens and ducks, have increasingly been kept in crowded barns and yards with minimal or no access at all to grass and sunlight throughout their lives. They are now mainly and routinely fed on concentrated food – corn and grain – often with growth hormones to speed up weight gain and antibiotics added to keep them disease-free. The fat in the meat from such animals loses its natural omega-3 to omega-6 balance entirely, so do the eggs from the chickens and ducks, and so does the milk from the cows. People who regularly eat such meat, eggs and dairy products are very likely to put on a lot of weight and become unable to lose much of it without enormous and continuous effort.

Back to how it should be

Grass, especially spring grass, is extra rich in omega-3 so that cows, grazing freely on plenty of grass in the fields most of the year, will produce milk, and therefore cream, butter and yoghurt, which is also rich in omega-3. In just the same way beef cattle, living mainly on grass, and chickens which are able to forage freely and eat grass and all kinds of seeds and bugs as they naturally like to do, will produce meat and eggs rich in omega-3. The perfect omega-3 to omega-6 balance will be there for the calves, for the baby chicks and for us.

What you can do to help yourself

- ♥ Eat fewer meat products and always ask for meat from free-range animals and eggs from organically fed free-range chickens.
- ♥ Only drink whole, organic milk. Skimmed and semi-skimmed milk has lost its essential fatty acid balance and some precious vitamins. Try to drink less milk anyway, it is not meant for the human body. It's meant for calves which have quite different needs and are many times the weight of a human baby or toddler.
- ♥ Make your own decisions about what you are going to eat and when, write a list and pin it up on the kitchen cupboard, where you can glance at it if you forget what you now know!

Here are a few ideas from people who have managed to pull themselves back from the brink of a severe weight problem.

> *'I made myself use a small-size plate that could not hold a huge meal – and decided no second helpings ever.'*

> *'I decided never to snack between meals, apart from fruit, raw carrots, cauliflower or celery. No burgers or hot dogs, ever. It was terrible at first but then I began to feel healthier and so much better after about six weeks. It made me feel really proud of myself!'*

'I tried to develop new interests to distract myself from eating, especially when I had been out and just come home – the worst moment of temptation. If I could get straight back to my dress-making or window-box gardening, or playing a game with my three-year-old, then my mind was kept off the bread bin and the jam pot!'

'I've stopped eating packaged, ready-made meals more often than once a week. I started teaching myself, for the first time, how to cook from fresh, whole foods, without adding fat or sugar and only a little salt. It seemed a bit tasteless at first till I started adding herbs, tomato puree, lemon juice or Indian spices.'

'I stopped buying any margarine or ready-made meals with "trans-fatty acids", "saturated fats" or "hydrogenated oils" listed in the nutritional information.'

'I bought organic butter and milk, free range or 'omega eggs' and meat whenever it was possible. It cost a bit more but that helped me too in a way. I had to buy less and eat less.'

'I fill a big jug of water as soon as I come downstairs in the morning and make sure it is empty by teatime.'

'I try to double the amount of vegetables on my plate and halve the potatoes, pasta and bread. I keep the protein bit – fish, eggs, meat, cheese – small too.'

'I push my buggy with my baby really fast, twice round the park – walking so fast it's almost running. He loves it and it's good for a laugh.'

'I also followed Paul McKenna's advice in his book, I Can Make You Thin. It really works!'

'I got my courage up and went swimming twice a week. The worst part was trying to buy a swimsuit big enough to get into. The first time I got in the pool, I had my eyes almost shut because I felt so shy and embarrassed. Also, it was impossible to climb up the vertical stepladder to get out. Luckily there were ordinary steps at the shallow end. I made myself swim one more length each visit until I was up to fifteen. Now I dare measure my waist every few weeks and feel very proud to see it going down steadily. One day soon I'll be able to stand on the scales!'

Obesity and pregnancy

Being obese and pregnant at the same time can be dangerous, both for mothers and for their babies. It can also set a pattern of being seriously overweight which is likely to continue from generation to generation.

If you are planning to have a baby, it matters more than you could possibly imagine to do everything you can, before you conceive, to be within a 'weight safety zone'. Ask your doctor about this. This way you will avoid some of the serious risks for yourself and your baby, which you would otherwise be facing throughout your pregnancy, the birth and in the years to follow. The problem is that 50% of pregnancies are unplanned and many women who are already obese are among this 50%. Any efforts to lose weight during the early months of pregnancy will have to be very carefully planned and monitored by your doctor, midwife or a nutritionist. More advice and help is becoming available.

At the other end of the scale are the equally serious risks to a pregnant woman and her unborn baby if she is anorexic and is not eating enough good food to absorb the nutrients she needs to keep herself healthy and to feed her growing infant. She may not have the strength to give birth naturally, nor recover from the birth easily and quickly – nor will she have enough breastmilk for her growing baby.

These are some of the questions that women ask their midwives and doctors:

Q   If I'm seriously overweight, will this prevent me from conceiving?

A   *Obesity can be a barrier – making it more difficult to conceive a baby.*

Q   How can I cope with the struggle of losing some weight now I find I am pregnant – without getting too stressed out and so harming my baby before he is born?

A   *Dieting to lose weight during pregnancy isn't advised. Eat whole, fresh organic foods as much as you can and avoid all high fat, salty and sugary food. Ask your doctor if you could see a registered dietician who has experience of working with pregnant mothers. Walk, swim and cycle as much as you can.*

Q   Will my pregnancy be normal?

A   *Sometimes everything will go normally but obesity definitely increases the chance of a miscarriage and also makes it more likely for a baby to be stillborn.*

Q   Will my baby grow too big in the womb because of my obesity?

A   *Not always, but the chances are high that he will be considerably overweight by six months' gestation and seriously overweight when he is born. This could make the birth longer and more difficult.*

Q   What are the risks for me now?

A   *Women who are obese when they become pregnant face many extra health hazards. There is an increased likelihood of diabetes, high blood pressure, heart disease, stroke, infections and sleeping problems. Bulky, fatty tissues round the neck disturb breathing, especially at night. This, in turn, increases the risk of falling asleep when driving a car which could cause an accident.*

Q   Is being so overweight going to make the birth more difficult?

A   *Usually yes – there will be much greater likelihood that you and your baby will need medical interventions of some kind during labour and the birth – and after the birth.*

Q   Will my baby be OK when I go into labour?

A   *It's more likely that your baby will need to be induced, need medical intervention during labour and be born by caesarean section. All this is because your labour is very likely to be held up during the first and the second stage because of less efficient contractions of your uterus. Your baby may be above normal birth weight and less likely to be in the best position for delivery.*

Q   How will it be after the birth?

A   *There is an increased risk of heavy bleeding, even haemorrhage, after the birth and this is always dangerous for a mother. It can be more difficult for obese mothers to begin and to continue breastfeeding.*

Q   Will I be able to lose weight after the birth?

A   *Obese mothers are more likely to continue gaining weight after the birth of their baby. You will need help and your own brave determination to persevere in your efforts to return to and keep to a healthy weight.*

We all get worried when a woman arrives on the ward in labour when she's seriously obese. We know that it will need more staff available than we have on the ward to get her safely through the birth and her baby breathing properly afterwards. We know that her baby is certain to be well above even a normal 'big baby' weight and that is always dangerous.
A maternity nurse

> *It's taking me ages to recover from the birth. It was so painful and difficult and carried on for more than 48 hours. I am not sure I have recovered yet because I still feel shattered and think about myself rather than my baby. That doesn't feel right.*
>
> **An obese mother with her seven-week-old baby who already weighs as much as a one-year-old**

A baby born large and overweight is likely to stay that way with all the heartache, struggle and poor health repeating itself for the next generation and the next. These children usually have low self-esteem and never get to feel really good about themselves. They fail to reach their potential and discover the best in themselves.

Babies and young children mimic their parents – what they say and what they do – because that's how they learn most things. If a mother has eating difficulties, if she is preoccupied by her weight, her dieting or her compulsive eating, her child is more than likely to pick up the fraught atmosphere that may develop around shopping, preparing and eating food.

Recovering from a Hard Birth

Every birth is different. Most births are straightforward and go at a steady pace, just as hoped and expected. However, just occasionally a birth is more like a long hard climb up a mountain in very rough weather. This can leave you feeling battered and exhausted. It can leave you feeling as shattered as if you have lost a boxing match... but with such a happy and life-changing reward that somehow you know you must and will recover.

A difficult or very long birth can also leave some mothers with very painful feelings and thoughts. This distress and sadness is hard to bear just at a time which should be of wonder, relief and joy.

If this has been your experience, you will need extra help, comfort and reassurance to recover from those painful memories. The best help usually comes from being able to share your difficult birth experiences with someone close to you. Talking right through it bit by bit, and again and again if you need to and being listened to with understanding for as long as it takes, is the best way to ease the distressing memories, to recover quickly, to begin to relax and give love to your baby.

An exhausted newborn

An overlong or hard birth may also mean coping with a distressed and crying baby for a while. A newborn baby may be so exhausted by long and powerful birth contractions that he will just sleep and sleep for the first few days. This can give everyone a false impression that this peace will continue, but the calm may suddenly be shattered in the next week or so if he is still feeling tense from the shock and fear – even pain – that may have almost overwhelmed him during the last stages of his birth.

Daily crying may start up as the only way he has – apart from suckling – of releasing the tension that built up in his tiny body over what may have been for him a painful, frightening and lonely experience for long hours.

The more a birth-shocked and crying baby can be

- held
- stroked slowly and gently all over, again and again every day
- walked around (the familiar rhythm)

- shussshed loudly and steadily (like the familiar sound he heard in the womb)
- smiled at
- talked and sung to (if you have been singing during your pregnancy)
- suckled whenever and as long as he wants
- the faster will be his recovery.

Suddenly he will begin to sleep peacefully again for hours between feeds. Suddenly he will be lying quietly in your arms, watching your eyes and your smile. You have done wonders!

Very occasionally the birth-shock carries on for longer, perhaps because the pressure on all the different plates of bones that make up his skull have been shifted during the birth and then failed to return to normal. A cranial osteopath is trained to put this problem right and can do so gently by fingertip touch. You could ask your midwife about the possibility of cranial osteopathic treatment for your baby.

A burden on Dad too

If the baby's father has been there during the labour and birth and been watching the exhaustion and distress being borne by the mum – maybe continuing during the next few weeks – he is likely to be feeling helpless and be suffering too. He will need the steadying comfort of being able to talk to someone with experience and understanding. Also to be able to find time every day to walk about, holding and soothing his child.

If this is so for you, you will find that the rhythm of walking about slowly with your baby in your arms every day for as long as possible at a stretch, will soon reduce your sense of helplessness and begin to change everything for the better. Walking outside in the fresh air, if it is warm and windless enough, is even more of a comfort than being indoors.

'Baby Blues' and Postnatal Depression

Babies draw love into themselves from looking at their mother's face. If their mother's face is blank and unsmiling because of postnatal depression – or drink or drugs – her interaction with her baby will be chaotic. The baby will first grow confused, then fearful and a short while later, angry. He will turn his face away again and again because there is no welcome and no joy – just sadness and emptiness. If wise and experienced medical as well as family help is not available instantly, that child's whole life will be under threat because of the damage that is being done to his loving spirit. It will begin to die like a plant without water and he may never fully recover.
A midwife in Newcastle, UK

'BABY BLUES'

Mild depression, sometimes called the 'baby blues', is very different from severe postnatal depression. These comparatively short-lived surges of emotional and physical exhaustion may suddenly come over you during the first weeks after the birth. They can make you feel distressed, weepy and upset, without any obvious cause. This is often just a short-term reaction to the dramas, expectations and celebrations around the birth. All that first excitement has suddenly died down, and you begin to feel lonely, especially with this entirely new responsibility in your arms. Your hormones are shifting from supporting the great physical demands of giving birth to settling into a new pattern for a nursing mother. It can make you feel very strange.

One way you can help yourself dispel the 'baby blues' is to concentrate totally – put your whole heart into – every small mundane thing you are doing: tidying stuff, cleaning, brushing your teeth, making a cuppa, as well as the big things like loving and talking to your baby, your children, your partner, your neighbour. This is a skill to practise in between resting whenever you can.

Occasionally, mothers suffer from prenatal depression during pregnancy but feel fine after the birth.

> *My husband helps me a lot but he doesn't understand what I'm feeling. He thinks it's just tiredness.*

Midwives will talk to expectant mothers and fathers about the symptoms of 'baby blues' and postnatal depression and what to do if they are affected. It is important to feel confident about asking for help after the birth and have some idea of what to do to find it.

However, some mums think that midwife and health visitor visits after birth focus only on how their baby is doing or give breastfeeding advice – not on how they are feeling, which is even more important! Where the birth rate has gone up and there is a current shortage of midwives and health visitors there is too little time for the kindness of listening and talking through your anxieties. Make sure you do talk to someone about how you are feeling if you are suddenly low, tearful and anxious.

Could you help yourself by finding a friend to talk to every day, also by trying to do less and rest more so you don't get over-tired? The 'baby blues' will soon pass.

Have I got postnatal depression?

> *For nearly a year I was so depressed. I don't think I smiled more than once a week and that was only for a second. I felt terrible. I wished that someone would notice but they didn't. Because I was caring for my baby OK – feeding her and changing her and all that – they probably thought I was OK too but I wasn't. I couldn't love her. Feeling shattered all the time stops you loving your baby.*

Postnatal depression (PND) is an illness. It can feel like the growth of an overwhelming sadness with no way to overcome it. It is also very hard to talk about it, yet talking about it to someone wise and full of care is the start of overcoming it.

> *If depression was a cancer it would be near the top of the list for deserving medical attention. The extent of human suffering in the world through depression is close behind the suffering of those with cancer.*
> **Dr Heidi Ledford**

Finding out the 'why' of developing severe depression is the first step to take. This means lots of memory exploration in your life through talking to anyone in your family – whatever generation – who you feel close to (and any professionals who know you well). This will help you understand something of the stresses and strains you have borne and which are affecting you now.

- What happened to me way back in my babyhood or childhood?
- What happened to me recently?
- Was I separated from my baby for the first few moments, hours or even days after birth?
- Have I felt very upset by something someone said to me?
- Am I fearful of what the future may hold for me?
- Am I able to eat enough fresh, whole food with all its vital nutrients, and drink plenty of water?

At its worst, postnatal depression can be so severe and overwhelming that it can take over your life – and therefore the life of your family. It can start up at any time during the first year after the birth of your baby. It means feeling so exhausted, helpless and depressed that you're forever in a state of panic and hardly able to function at all *or to love and care for your baby.*

This is the description by a dad of the depression he also felt after the birth of his daughter:

> *It's like having nothing but adrenaline and panic pumping through you.*
> *It's like being a computer with all the billions of bits of data which add up to 'me' infected by a super-bug and disappearing.*
> *It's like being a carrot being peeled so you're standing naked in the wind.*
> *It's like having a broken neck and being told to get a grip on yourself.*
> **Giles Andreae**

Are any of these symptoms yours?

- You get irritated and angry, and try to avoid talking to anyone.
- You feel ashamed to admit anything is wrong.
- You feel utterly exhausted and lacking in energy.
- You can't enjoy or be interested in anything.
- You lie awake worrying half the night.
- You wake each morning with fear and panic and with tears running down your cheeks.
- You lose your appetite and forget to eat, or start overeating and putting on weight.
- You feel anxious all the time about your baby's health and weight, that you aren't looking after him properly, and that he doesn't love you.
- You have to really force yourself to smile at him and talk to him.
- You may feel a great hopelessness – that things will never get better.
- You may sometimes find that you can't breathe properly, that your heart is thumping and that you are sweating – like having a panic attack.

It's not your fault! You will get better. You need lots of help. You can't manage on your own. Tell someone who knows about postnatal depression and ask them to help you. Keep asking!

> *'I'm scared I'm going to end up hitting or shaking my baby.'*
>
> *'One sentence keeps on going round and round in my head all day long: "I shouldn't be feeling like this".'*

Each person is different, the symptoms are different and so is the length of time that postnatal depression may hold you down, clamped in misery.

Much more has been researched and discovered about the earliest background causes behind the likelihood of an individual mother developing postnatal depression. And it is now recognised to be a real emergency which must be treated very seriously and without any delay.

> *I got more and more bad tempered and emotional. I felt alone, even when Mum was there to help me. I felt useless, worthless and ashamed of how I was feeling. I couldn't concentrate and I couldn't sleep. I didn't want even to look at my baby. Smiling at him was impossible.*

In some hospitals, severe postnatal depression can be treated in a special mother and baby unit.

Lots of possible causes

There is almost never a single cause of depression. The most usual, known causes are:

* The lack of friendship, support and the presence of a known and trusted midwife or doula during pregnancy and throughout the birth – and afterwards.
* A lack of peace and privacy during labour.
* Your hormones have not yet rebalanced after the birth.
* The huge, life-changing event of childbirth, or another, recent traumatic event, such as relationship breakdown, moving house or bereavement.
* A birth which felt out of control and frightening, or you were seriously affected by complications during labour, or you had to have an emergency caesarean section.
* The non-stop demands of looking after your newborn baby, especially if he cries a lot and is difficult to soothe and to feed.
* Acute shortage of sleep and what this does to your brain and your heart.
* A big upheaval in your life – like having a baby – can bring about temporary chemical changes in your brain which result in symptoms of depression.

- The loss of companionship at work and friends able to visit.
- Living with a lower income than before.
- An underactive thyroid.
- The subconscious resurfacing of some of the pain and panic which you perhaps felt at the time of your own birth. It might help to ask your mum what your birth was like.

Babies reflect their mother's feelings

In no time at all they learn to recognise happiness, sadness, surprise and depression on their mother's face, and start trying to change the blankness in her face back to smiles by reaching out, making noises and gazing to get attention. If this fails, babies get depressed too, look away, cry in protest and begin to act wary of their mother.

> *The first four months of my daughter's life were overshadowed by my depression and now she is a toddler I'm sure she has grown withdrawn and anxious as a result of her experience of feeling unloved and 'deserted' by me when she was very little. I thought it would all go away and I never asked for help.*
> **Shona**

Getting help

There are increasingly effective ways now of bringing postnatal depression steadily to an end.

There are different kinds of perinatal mental health services in different areas able to provide the information, advice and care you need. Ask your midwife, health visitor or doctor.

From 2012, NHS England began training and building up the numbers of mental health specialist GPs, specialist mental health midwives and health visitors.

Maybe you will be referred to the Family Nurse Partnership for support or a local children's centre running courses for mothers with anxiety and depression.

Mind, a charity, offers advice and support in the field of mental health and provides a specific section on postnatal depression.

www.mind.org.uk/information-support/types-of-mental-health-problems/postnatal-depression-and-perinatal-mental-health/?gclid=EAIaIQobChMIrIKvo8zP1wIVxrftCh3Teg2LEAAYASAAEgJ4sfD_BwE#.WhQSb1Vl_c

Maternal Mental Health is Everyone's Business
www.everyonesbusiness.org.uk

Family Action's Perinatal Project provides trained volunteer befrienders to undertake home visits and help run support groups locally. These support groups help new mothers with family relationships, bonding with their new baby and general parenting skills. They provide important social, emotional and parenting support for you.
www.family-action.org.uk

PANDAS Foundation is a charity supporting families suffering from perinatal mental health illness. They provide a helpline (0843 2898401 from 9am – 8pm), support groups and online advice.
www.pandasfoundation.org.uk

Mumsnet provides a wealth of links and articles on postnatal depression to assist you in finding help.
www.mumsnet.com

Netmums will give you information, support and friendship. You can chat to other mums or a health visitor online about postnatal depression, learn self-help exercises and take the '10 steps to recovery'. And you can learn about the latest research into mums' maternal health.
www.netmums.com

NCT (National Childbirth Trust) provides information and help for stressed and anxious mums. They run 'Relax, Stretch and Breathe' classes. www.nct.org.uk

Never forget how much people care about you and your baby and want to help. Never forget that you will recover completely.

Born Disabled

When a baby is born with physical defects or is malformed in some way parents' reactions can be turbulent and desperate. Suddenly, often without any warning, a great burden of shock, grief and worry falls upon them. Instantly they realise what huge adjustments they will need to understand and to make in caring for this baby, at the same time carrying tremendous anxieties about all the years ahead. Who would be there to show them and help them and share the burden?

Feeling shattered by so much uncertainty and often a deep sadness – even uncalled-for guilt – causes some parents to draw back from their child so that the normal warm bonding processes of the first few weeks is seriously held back. This is like starvation for their baby.

For other parents, the pity of it so fills their heart that their outpouring of love for this different child – with all the challenges they will have to face – takes over and instantly builds an unbreakable bond with their child.

www.nct.org.uk/pregnancy/babies-disabilities
www.gov.uk/help-for-disabled-child
http://raisingchildren.net.au/articles/disabilities_your_feelings.html
www.littlemiraclescharity.org.uk/

Abortion

This appendix, about a very emotional issue, is for you *only* if you have been thinking you might have an abortion (termination of your pregnancy)... or are being pressurised into having an abortion... or have had an abortion... or know a friend who has talked to you about having an abortion herself.

> *I still feel very sad when I think of what might have been... How my little girl would have been 20 years old by now and I wonder what she would have been like. But I know I made the right decision at the time and I had good friends and my sister to talk to. My boyfriend was upset and we later parted, but I knew it wouldn't have worked. My life would have been different. I can't put the clock back but I know I did the best thing I could at the time.*
> **Rosemary, a lawyer**

Whatever the case, the thoughts, the feelings and the decision made – either way – need to be shared with someone trustworthy and loving who will not judge nor accuse, nor turn their back on you. If you are loved and supported through the decision to have an abortion, your recovery is likely to be more complete.

A secret abortion

Alternatively, the loss of your baby through a secret abortion can come back and haunt you at unexpected moments in your life. A secret abortion can hurt your inner spirit – the spark which is *you* – perhaps even into your old age. Could you tell the story to someone who loves you even now, if that is possible?

All unwanted pregnancies which lead to abortion, even if at the time you felt relieved and grateful for it, do need to be shared with someone you love and trust. However, some women find it impossible to talk to anyone about their pregnancy and their decision to have an abortion – not their parents, nor their sister, nor their boyfriend, nor a close friend from school or work. If this is so for you, would you be able to consider sharing your troubled thoughts with a priest or an elder in your community?

There may be good reasons for keeping your abortion secret but this is an extra burden of loneliness to bear. It might help to keep a journal instead and write down your thoughts and feelings as you make your decisions, and to continue writing your feelings down for at least a year, or until things seem close to normal again. By doing this, you are acknowledging, accepting and respecting the decisions you have made.

> *I was 15 when I had an abortion. At the time I kept it a secret from my mum and dad. I wish I'd told them, even though it would have caused a big row. I'm married and have a family but I live every day wishing I'd kept my baby if I could have done that.*
> **Penny, 35 years old**

Sometimes, the buried sadness can 'grow back' rather than fade over the years – particularly if the abortion has been kept secret. Some women come to feel sudden little stabs in the heart as if they had wounded a part of themselves by taking away the chance of a life for a tiny new soul, a real person... and a future that cannot now be.

If the distress you feel does not recede and is affecting your relationships and your work, please do search out and ask for help through your GP or the internet. You will need to find someone who is trained and expert in giving emotional and psychological support.

> *We already had 3 children. I was pressured into abortion by my husband... I went through with it and it was such a horrible experience. I felt so alone and guilty. He showed no emotion and as soon as we came out of the clinic he wasn't interested in me at all. This drove me deep in depression... I always think about what if I had gone with my own decision to keep it.*
> **Anon**

> *My girlfriend and I have been together for almost 2 years now. Recently we just found out that she is 2 months pregnant which makes me very happy that I'm gonna be a father. The problem is that we knew about the pregnancy a month ago but she has not really accepted it and yesterday she told me that she is thinking of abortion. OK but I honestly don't support the idea as I'm already in love with my unborn child. But I kind of feel selfish as I have already graduated with my degree and am working while she is in her first year at the university. She cries every day and I don't know what to do. All I know is that if I let her go for abortion I don't think I'll ever forgive myself for that. I want to be a father and I'm definitely prepared for that, financially and emotionally. What can I do to help her accept and be happy with the situation?*
> **John**

Sadness can gather sadness

The loss of your baby by your own, lonely choice can also bring up again other powerful feelings of loss which you have experienced in your life and have been carrying with you perhaps ever since you were a child. This could have been the death of a beloved grandparent, or a close friend or a pet or just painful memories of feeling abandoned or neglected or unloved sometimes by your own parents. The 'losses' in your life may all come together now and be added to the big loss of an abortion, even if it had not felt like that at the time. This load on your heart can keep bobbing up to depress you, or fill you with an undercurrent of sadness, regardless of good things going on around you.

If this buried grief does keep interfering in your life like this or with that of anyone you know, it is essential to find someone who is trained, experienced and understanding to help heal the memories and get your life back to normal.

Sharona had the faith in herself to hang onto her baby against all the odds – as she describes below:

> I was 22 when I found out I was pregnant. I was an alcoholic and drug abuser, I was getting evicted from my residence, and wasn't even sure who the father of my child was. Both guys were also drug addicts and drinking heavily. My future for my baby and for me looked very dim, but I knew I couldn't give it up in abortion or adoption. I just knew that this was the situation I was in and I needed to do all I could to provide for this innocent life that grew inside of me. I moved in with my mum and a few months later out came Antonio Lee, a healthy 7lb 8oz bundle of joy. I did figure out who the father was and while I was still pregnant he went to a rehab and got help.

Remembering and honouring

If you continue to feel sorrowful after having an abortion, or a termination of your pregnancy for whatever reason, some kind of ritual can help. It can help and comfort you if you can do something which acknowledges what has happened, which gives a name to the child who you have lost and which asks for forgiveness. If you feel guilty, you must feel forgiven and at peace once more.

Some mothers sing a song that means a great deal to them, as if they are singing to their lost baby... some mothers dance to allow the music and movement to soothe them and to honour their lost baby... some parents find a wild and beautiful place to be for a while and perhaps light a candle or plant a tree. Some mothers, with or without the father of their baby, ask for a blessing from their priest or perhaps support a children's charity or a humanitarian project, in memory of their lost child.

I had an abortion when I was at university. I was scared a baby would ruin my life and my career. After that, I had trouble with my sex life. It was later that I had counselling and realised that the abortion was affecting my relationships. The thing that helped me a lot was to have a 'memorial ceremony'. I lit a big candle with flowers round it, and said all I was feeling out loud as if my lost baby was there with me. I told him again and again 'I'm sorry'. 'Please forgive me.' 'Thank you.' 'I love you.' From then on, the grief began to fade away and I began to recover myself.
Cheryl, 25

If you are distressingly and unexpectedly pregnant and finding it hard to make a decision on your own and are unable to talk to your parents or anyone else close to you, here are four experienced organisations able to support and help you:

Stand Up Girl
www.standupgirl.com

Brook Young People (for under 25s)
Tel: 0808 802 1234
www.brook.org.uk/pregnancy/abortion

Marie Stopes, 24-hour helpline
Tel: 0845 300 8090
www.mariestopes.org.uk/women/abortion

Life (Pregnancy Support)
Tel: 0800 915 4600
www.lifecharity.org.uk

What If my baby dies?

Miscarriage

Losing a baby in the early stages of pregnancy is very common. However early a miscarriage happens, the distress that comes with it can cause deep sadness and depression to an expectant dad as well as to an expectant mum. One in six pregnancies ends in miscarriage. However, losing a baby that is over seven months' gestation or full term can be a very different situation and is a stillbirth. Usually, the longer you carry your baby the greater the sense of loss and bereavement will be and the more confused and desperate you may feel, perhaps without any of the right words to describe your feelings and so help you with the pain.

Stillborn babies and babies who die soon after birth

Very rarely, a baby may be born too early or meet such severe difficulties during the birth that he does not survive. A baby might be born with physical problems that make life unsustainable for more than a few hours, or days, or weeks.

Facing this anguish with all the emotions, hopes and plans that you had for nine months, gone forever, is truly devastating. You feel you will never smile again.

But professional help will be there, close at hand, to share the shocking pain and grief, to listen and to guide you through the hours and days ahead.

There are some things which must be done in the first hours and which might help to steady you.

There will be some medical choices which now have to be made. Some of these will be your choices and some of them will not be, in which case the reasons for these medical decisions will be explained to you. There will be time to discuss and think about your choices, and your decisions will be supported.

Simple coping strategies to get through the days will be suggested and discussed with you and very practical ideas offered to help you, such as writing down simple sentences, on a notepad, to look at again and again. These practical ideas are to give you back control and help you to be gentle with yourself.

There are also those who have borne the same desolation in their own lives and are therefore able to understand the depth of your shock and grief. They will be able to listen to you and support you as soon as you contact them (see the list of books and organisations at the end of this appendix).

Because of present-day prenatal care, particularly scanning, parents usually know in advance if their baby has a medical problem which could prove life-threatening. But for all parents the loss of their baby, during or soon after birth, is a desperate shock. There is so much hope, anticipation, expectation and joy at the birth of a baby that the distress of an unexpected death is terrible beyond words.

A baby's death is out of tune with life. If it happens to your baby then there are no rules, no precedents and nothing that is going to make the loss bearable. All that there ever can be is eventual acceptance, through understanding what happened, and through the comfort of being with people you love and who care deeply about you and your baby. There will be other people around you too, who will walk beside you through this nightmare. They will be able to make such an experience a little easier to bear by helping you make the practical and medical choices that could be important for your peace of mind later. You will be gently informed about these, and involved in all decisions relating to your baby.

A mother has a right to feel exquisitely bad, to cry, to scream, to close her eyes and shut out the world, to share or to be silent about this death that should be a new life. This beginning is not right. It is not gentle. But it was a beginning and this cannot be lost or wiped away. This baby can be remembered and cherished.

In just the same way as healthy newborn babies are left with Mum and Dad, skin-to-skin, on their mother's belly, most parents will want to spend as many hours as they need, holding, cuddling, stroking and talking to their lost baby. This can still happen. Your baby can be washed and dressed beautifully, then held in your arms, or laid on the bed or in his crib if you are at home.

> *Two young parents whose first child, a little girl, died a few moments after she was born wrote the following week to James Blunt, the singer/songwriter. They told him how 'You're Beautiful' was their favourite song and how they had both sung it to their unborn baby many times during the pregnancy. They then described how they had sat together and walked up and down for hours in the maternity unit, just after the birth and her death, holding her in their arms and singing 'You're Beautiful' to her. They wrote to tell James what comfort his song had given them and to thank him.*

As time starts to move again and you have to find ways of getting through the days you can use ideas that others have found helped them.

You may want to talk, perhaps to somebody you don't know at all, but somebody who knows exactly how bad it is. Do this. Trust your instincts about who you want to talk with. Say it all, say everything, say it again and again or say nothing. You will know what might help you.

There may be some tiny things that will make a difference when days are black and nights are blacker.

Use the name you chose for your baby. Refer to your baby as the complete person he is despite the fact that he died. This way you give him the importance and respect he deserves. Use his name and he will have lived. He will have his rightful place and other people will take their lead from you.

For a while, keep close to you something that touched him, that wrapped him, that was next to him. If you have a picture of him, then look at it and keep looking. Ask someone close to you to make copies of it or even do a small drawing so that his image cannot be lost to you, now that you cannot see him nor hold him. You can ask the midwife if it is possible to have a tiny clay handprint and footprint made for you. These will also give you something special to show to people if you want to talk about the baby you cannot now share in any other way.

One day, as the grief begins to soften – as it will do in time – you will come to know that his spirit is there with you, inside you, in your heart and in your mind, and always will be.

The Birth and Death of My Baby

I carried the baby until week 37 and then I went into labour 3 weeks early but I still felt all was well. The baby was born 10 hours later in hospital after an easy labour. She was immediately seen to have spina bifida and several consultants were called. I looked into her eyes and knew she wanted to die. She stayed in the special care baby unit where I spent all the time I could with her until she died. She was 5 days old.

My husband had to get a birth certificate and a death certificate at the same time. It was way beyond my ability to deal with that. At first I denied my grief and tried to be normal. I stared at other people's babies in prams and felt desperately sad. I had given up my work and although my husband and my parents gave me all their support, everyone else seemed to want to get things back to normal instead of acknowledging the loss.

But, being hurried back into normality can make the sense of unreality and despair greater than ever. Like it never happened or better to forget it.

I had a few photographs of Katherine that had been taken in the hospital. That really helped. She was beautiful with dark hair and very pretty even though she had hydrocephalus.

I tried to conceive again immediately as a way of moving on and miscarried again. Help came about a year later. I had some nutritional help and also grief counselling and I felt I really was beginning to get over the losses. I never conceived again.

All I can say is, it really helps to talk, it really helps to cry with someone else and it really helps to be with other babies and let them heal our hearts. I now work with babies as a craniosacral therapist and find I am mother to hundreds of babies. As I love and care for them they become like my own.
Claire Dolby RCST

Cot death

Very rarely, a baby left sleeping and seemingly healthy and fine in every way will stop breathing and die without any obvious cause. This is called cot death or Sudden Infant Death Syndrome (SIDS). Cot death is the sudden and unexpected death of a baby aged less than a year and usually under six months. Very rarely, the baby may be over a year old. Often no specific cause can be found, despite detailed medical investigations.

Less than half of 1% of around 700,000 babies born each year in the UK die from completely unexplained causes. The number is falling every year, as more parents become aware of what the risks are. Babies are at their most vulnerable during the first three months – the period when they should ideally still be inside you, in the safety of the womb, while all their 'systems' mature a little more. If they have been born prematurely or are of low birth weight, the risk will be greater.

The overwhelming loss of a cot death can be more shattering for parents than any other way of losing a baby because it can leave them imagining that it somehow could have been their fault that their baby died. The anguish is therefore indescribable and for some parents can last for years. It needs enormous courage to overcome such sadness and then to stay calm and reassured when the next baby is born, both for his sake and for their own.

Many years of careful research into the unexpected deaths of young babies has begun to uncover some of the causes, though by no means all of them. The cause might be a previous unknown problem that the baby was born with, such as an undiagnosed heart condition or because of a breakdown of the part of the baby's brain which controls breathing, heart rate, blood pressure, temperature. Cot death might also be caused by serious illness from fast-acting bacteria. It is now known that some babies have died as a result of an invisible and particularly virulent virus. There might be other causes. Research continues.

Reducing the risks

Back-in-the-womb conditions as far as possible for your baby give the best protection of all from cot death in the early weeks. This means keeping close day and night and skin-to-skin contact for as many hours in the twenty-four as possible. Keeping as close as this to your baby at night helps you to care for him more easily if he shows signs of being unwell. You can tell straight away whether his temperature is soaring or whether he is shivering.

Many other things can be done to reduce the risk of cot death, however slight that risk is, if you follow this advice about the best sleeping conditions for your baby.

- ♥ Keep your baby close beside you or another caring adult, day and night, for the first six months. Your bodily closeness is his best protection. During the day, carry him against your chest in a sling or baby carrier.
- ♥ Breastfeed your baby unless this is impossible – especially, and often during the night – whenever he shows he needs to suck.
- ♥ Never allow anyone to smoke in the same room as your baby.
- ♥ Never smoke at all as parents. The second-hand smoke in your breath and on your skin and clothing will affect his breathing.
- ♥ Never lie your baby on his front to sleep – but start him on his back just for the first few weeks. Once he is sturdy enough to move his head easily from side to side he can be put down, curled up on one side or the other. He will probably show you that this is the position he likes best to sleep in. It is the same with most adults. Sleeping in these different positions will also protect your baby from developing a flattened or misshapen skull (plagiocephaly).
- ♥ Always lay your baby in a crib or a cot with his feet almost touching the end so he cannot wriggle down under the covers and cover his mouth and nose.
- ♥ Do not sleep with your baby in bed with you for the first two months or so if he was premature or small and frail at birth. Use a Bednest instead (see Chapter 9) or any bedside crib that allows your baby to sleep right beside you, at the same level and within sight and touch of each other.
- ♥ Try to keep the room temperature between 16 and 20 degrees centigrade. If your baby is sweating or his tummy feels hot take off a layer of his clothes or bed covers.
- ♥ Keep duvets, pillows, radiators and hot water bottles away from your baby.
- ♥ Take your baby's outdoor clothes off as soon as you get inside.
- ♥ Telephone for medical advice if your baby seems ill – not just showing some signs of a cold.

If you feel very anxious when you become pregnant again after losing a baby through cot death, a breathing monitor called CONI (Care of the Next Infant) will sound an alarm to alert you if your baby stops breathing for more than twenty seconds.

www.lullabytrust.org.uk/coni

When I look back to the day our daughter died, I think mostly of two things. Wanting to stay and hold her and never, ever let her go. And wishing the hospital chaplain had been with me after she died. I would have liked a chaplain to have been there because I feel his training and instinct would have been

to give me all his attention, care and support. Whether I believed in God or not, he would have known how much I needed spiritual comfort and some kind of peace however impossible that seemed then. I would like not to have felt alone in my despair and confusion. I would have liked him to have taken my daughter from me and held her in his arms when I had to leave her.
Sue

A SPECIAL SERVICE OF BLESSING OR BAPTISM

Parents who have suffered the death of their baby often want to know if they would be able to have a special blessing or baptism for their baby in hospital, or at home if it has been a home birth. Here is one example of a ceremony of naming and blessing and also a service of baptism for your baby. These are here for you to look at, to give you ideas. You could change the wording as you wish.

A ceremony of naming and blessing

First of all you will want to choose who will lead this ceremony for you – maybe the hospital chaplain or a senior midwife or close older friend?

At the end of this naming and blessing ceremony, there are also some poems and readings which you might like to choose from. It is suggested that whatever you choose are read after the blessing, before the closing words.

Whoever is conducting the ceremony invites everyone in the room to sit round the parents, one of whom is holding their baby.

Everyone in the room is welcome and we thank you for being here to share your love and support for the parents of this child (the name you have given your baby). This ceremony is one of dedication, love and respect. It is also to say 'goodbye' and to bless him (her).

Please tell me what name you have given to your baby. In naming him we celebrate one of life's continuing miracles, the birth of a human being. We rejoice that this child has been born into the loving arms of his parents. This child's name will be spoken aloud. It will be whispered. It will be shouted, cried, perhaps sung and written down by family, friends, neighbours and maybe by other children and grandchildren.

We give this child a name in this ceremony because, by doing so, we tell each other that he (she) is an individual, a unique and a separate person with a dignity, spirit and a life of his (her) own. We name this beautiful baby (the name you have chosen). We all bless him (her) before we say goodbye to him (her) at this saddest of times.

Death unites us all in several ways. (Name)'s death for a time asks that each one of us put aside our work and all other concerns and pleasures to mourn together in our shared love for this child, whose life has just ended. He (she) has already had a great influence on your lives (name parents). This influence will not end.

Your grief is a powerful sign that death cannot take from us the most precious of treasures, namely love. It is the tears of love that flow the fullest, the pain of love that aches the deepest, the feelings of love that move us most actively, and make us grieve so deeply for the loss of one so young. Remembering a baby who has died touches our hearts and stays in our hearts all our lives.

Shall we sit in silence for a moment or two and then each of us might come to touch, to give our own silent blessing and say goodbye to (name). I will end this ceremony by blessing you all.

Here is one example of a blessing to end your memorial ceremony, but you might like to choose another or write your own.

May the Lord bless you and keep you. May the Lord make his face to shine upon you, and be gracious to you. May the Lord lift up his countenance upon you, and give you peace.

READINGS AND POEMS FOR YOU TO CHOOSE FROM

We Cannot Care for You the Way We Wanted

We cannot care for you the way we wanted,
or cradle you or listen for your cry;
but, separated as we are by silence,
love will not die.
We cannot watch you grow into your childhood
and find a new uniqueness every day;
but special as you would have been among us,
you still will stay.
So through the mess of anger, grief and tiredness,
through tensions which are not yet reconciled,
we hold you, name and bless you
our precious child.

There is a Word

There is a word of grief the sounding token.
There is a word bejeweled with bright tears.
The saddest word fond lips have ever spoken,
A little word that breaks the chain of years.
Its utterance must ever bring emotion,
The memories it crystals cannot die.
'Tis known in every land, on every ocean,
It is
Goodbye.

There are Griefs So Gentle

There are griefs so gentle in their very nature that it would be worse than
false heroism to refuse them a tear. Of this kind are the deaths of infants...
Those who have lost an infant are never, as it were, without an infant child.
Their other children grow up to manhood and womanhood, and suffer all the
changes of mortality; but this one alone is rendered an immortal child; for
death has arrested it with his kindly harshness, and blessed it into an eternal
image of youth and innocence.
James Henry Leigh Hunt

A Butterfly

A butterfly lights beside us like a sunbeam.
And for a brief moment its glory and beauty belong to our world.
But then it flies on again, and though we wish it could have stayed,
We are so thankful to have seen it.
We Bereaved Are Not Alone
We bereaved are not alone.
We belong to the largest company in all the world, the company of those who
have known suffering.
When it seems that our sorrow is too great to be borne, let us think of
the great family of the heavy hearted into which our grief has given us
entrance, and inevitably, we will feel about us their arms, their sympathy, their
understanding.
Believe, when you are most unhappy, that there is something for you to do
in the world.
So long as you can sweeten another's pain, life is not in vain.
Helen Keller

The Truest Words of All: I Will Not Forget You

The truest words of all: I will not forget you.
You are in my waking thoughts,
my sweetest memories, my dearest dreams.
I will not forget you.
You have touched my soul, opened my eyes,
changed my very experience of the universe.
I will not forget you.
I see you in the flowers, the sunset,
the sweep of the horizon
and all things that stretch to infinity.
I will not forget you.
I have carved you on the palm of my hand.
I carry you with me forever.

A baptism service

Sometimes an annual remembrance service is held in the hospital chapel or the local church for all babies who have died in the hospital. This service is for all denominations and for everyone. Someone will be able to tell you about this.

SOURCES OF INFORMATION, ADVICE, COMFORT AND HELP

The first place to start is with your family, relations, friends and your midwife for understanding and comfort. Then look for some experienced professional help. Whether your baby was stillborn or died through cot death or any other reason during babyhood, the following organisations can give you information, advice and support:

♥ **The Child Death Helpline**
   Run in partnership with the Great Ormond Street Children's Hospital.
   Freephone 0800 282986
   www.childdeathhelpline.org.uk/

♥ **The Compassionate Friends**:
   Run local group meetings, make home visits and have a library of books and videos that may be able to comfort and help you to heal. Their helpline is manned by a bereaved parent every day of the year.
   Tel: 08451 232304 from 10am-6pm and 6.30-10.30pm
   www.tcf.org.uk

♥ **SANDS** (the Stillbirth and Neonatal Society)
Can offer you and other members of your family support if your baby died during your pregnancy, or you had to make the difficult decision to end your pregnancy. In the same way, their support is there for you if your baby was stillborn or died soon after birth.
Tel: 0207 7436 5881
www.uk-sands.org

♥ **Babyloss**
Runs online forums for parents who have lost their baby.
www.babyloss.com

Books to comfort and steady you

♥ *Michael Rosen's Sad Book*
Author: Michael Rosen
Publisher: Walker Books Ltd, London, 2004
Michael Rosen writes about the loss of his own son, Eddie. He writes about his sadness, how it affects him and some of the things he does to try to cope with it.

♥ *Living with Leo*
Author: Mario Di Clemente
Publisher: Bosun-Publications, Shepperton, 2004
Leonardo Di Clemente died the day after he was born. His father, Mario, has written movingly of his experience of prospective fatherhood and the distress of bereavement. Twelve letters written over a year, from a father to his son, tell the story of Mario's life with Leo: of the excitement and anticipation, the grief and loss, and perhaps most important of all, the emergence of strength and hope.

♥ *Miscarriage: Women's Experiences and Needs*
Author: Christine Moulder
This sympathetic and helpful book explores the many different ways in which women physically experience miscarriage and emotionally react to it. Every aspect of miscarriage is covered, including difficult issues that are often avoided. The book also provides good practical guidelines for professionals, based on what women themselves say they find helpful.

♥ *Just My Reflection –*
Helping Parents to Do Things Their Way When Their Baby Dies
Author: Sister Frances Dominica

♥ ***When a Baby Dies***
Authors: Nancy Kohner and Alix Henley
Parents who have lost a baby tell their stories – how they felt, how others have helped them and how they helped themselves.

♥ ***Brief Lives***
Author: Christine Moulder
Brief Lives is an anthology of parents' writings about their experiences of the death of their baby.

♥ ***Empty Cradle, Broken Heart: Surviving the Death of Your Baby***
Author: Deborah L. Davis
Especially for parents who struggle with anger, guilt and despair after such tragedy. There is also a special chapter for fathers as well as a chapter on protective parenting to help anxious parents enjoy their precious living children.

♥ ***Fathers Feel Too***
Author: Andrew Don
A book for men by men on coping with the death of a baby.

♥ ***Angel Catcher for Kids***
Author: Amy Eldon
Suggests ways to help a child cope with the painful and often confusing process of grieving for a lost baby brother or sister or anyone else of any age who has been close to them.

♥ ***Stewart's Tree***
Author: Cathy Campbell
A book for brothers and sisters aged 3+ when a baby dies shortly after birth.

Resources To Help You

This additional list of resources gives you details of helplines, books, DVDs, products and organisations which might be able to give you useful and comforting advice and help.

HELPLINES

BfN (The Breastfeeding Network)
Helpline: 0300 100 0312
www.breastfeedingnetwork.org.uk
Also help in Welsh and Polish
BfN Supporterline in Bengali / Sylheti: 0300 456 2421

Cry-sis
Helpline: 08451 228 669
www.cry-sis.org.uk
Advice and support for families with excessively crying, sleepless and demanding babies.

Home Start
Helpline: 0116 464 5490
www.home-start.org.uk
Volunteers give support, friendship and practical help to young families in their own homes.

La Leche League, GB
Helpline: 0345 120 2918
www.laleche.org.uk
Telephone counselling for breastfeeding and weaning. Mother-to-mother support groups, help and information.

Mothers for Mothers
Helpline: 0117 975 6006
www.mothersformothers.co.uk
Postnatal depression support group, giving support, advice, information and most of all a listening ear.

National Childbirth Trust (NCT)
Tel: 0300 330 0700
www.nct.org.uk
Antenatal classes and local postnatal support groups for parents.

SANDS (Stillbirth and Neonatal Death Society)
Helpline: 0808 164 3332
helpline@sands.org.uk
www.sands.org.uk

TAMBA (Twins and Multiple Births Association)
Helpline: 0800 138 0509
asktwinline@tamba.org.uk
www.tamba.org.uk
Gives encouragement and support to parents of twins or multiple births.

ORGANISATIONS

Active Birth Centre
Tel: 0207 281 6760
www.activebirthcentre.com
Pregnancy yoga, antenatal courses, early parenting and postnatal classes. Helping you trust your instincts when you give birth.

Best Beginnings
www.bestbeginnings.org.uk
Founder and Chief Executive Alison Baum. Support for parents to give every child in the UK the best start in life through innovative evidence-based resources including award-winning free Apps.

BLISS
Freephone: 0808 801 032
www.bliss.org.uk
A charity for sick or premature babies. Research, support and help for parents and neonatal professionals.

Birthing the Future
www.birthingthefuture.org
Suzanne Arms' vision and wisdom towards creating a better world through the baby-mother bond.

Brazelton Centre in Great Britain

Tel: 01223 245791

www.brazelton.co.uk

Helping parents to understand their baby's intelligence and individuality and to communicate with them from birth.

CARE (Christian Action Research and Education)

Tel: 0207 233 045

www.care.org.uk

Christian concern for the value of human life and the importance of marriage and strong, happy families.

Doula UK

Tel: 0871 4333103

www.doula.org.uk

Doulas support the whole family to have a positive experience of pregnancy, birth and early weeks with the new baby. Find a doula near you through their website.

Fathers-To-Be International

Tel: 01892 890614

www.fatherstobe.org

Supporting expectant and new dads by reinforcing their confidence in themselves and their relationship with their partners, their babies and the health professionals caring for the family.

Fertility Network UK

Tel: 01424 732361

www.fertilitynetworkuk.org

Fertility Network UK provides free and impartial support, advice, information and understanding for anyone affected by fertility issues.

All their services are FREE.

Information on Paternity and Maternity leave

www.gov.uk/pay-leave-for-parents

Will give information on paternity leave and maternity leave and other rights such as flexible working and adoption rights.

Lullaby Trust

Tel: 0808 802 6868

www.lullabytrust.org.uk

Aims to promote infant health and prevent sudden unexpected deaths in infancy. Befriending support for bereaved parents.

Note: Right from the Start is concerned about one aspect of their excellent guidance. Their advice 'to sleep newborn babies always on their backs' is sometimes not helpful. Unless they are very premature, babies should be laid down to sleep in three changing positions, either curled up in the foetal position on their left or their right side, or on their back. This avoids the earliest stress for babies of their spine being suddenly stretched out flat for the first time, for quite long periods. It also avoids the risk of developing positional plagiocephaly (flat head syndrome). Most babies, as soon as they are strong enough, will find their own favourite sleeping position anyway. Even more important than a baby's sleeping position is being within touch and breath reach of Mum, Dad or a mother figure for almost all of the twenty-four hours of the day for the first five to six months.

The Lullaby Trust provides an excellent little booklet, 'Babycheck: Is your baby really ill?'. This was developed by a team of paediatricians in Cambridge. It gives you nineteen checkpoints and a chart to help you discover whether or not your baby is ill.

www.lullabytrust.org.uk/wp-content/uploads/baby-check-2015.pdf

International Association of Infant Massage – UK
Tel: 0208 989 9597
www.iaim.org.uk
Can put you in touch with qualified infant massage instructors.

Association for Infant Mental Health
www.aimh.org.uk
Research and the importance of support for parents towards their babies brain development and mental health.

Natal Hypnotherapy
Tel: 01252 716859
www.natalhypnotherapy.co.uk
The Natal Hypnotherapy Programme is a self-hypnosis course which you listen to at home during your pregnancy. The course helps you overcome fear and be more relaxed, preparing you for birth. You learn breathing, relaxation and visualisation skills which can help reduce pain, shorten labour and reduce intervention. It is offered in various formats – MP3, USB stick and an online course.

National Childbirth Trust (NCT)
Tel: 0300 330 0700
www.nct.org.uk
Antenatal classes and local postnatal support groups for parents.

National Health Service
www.nhs.uk/conditions/pregnancy-and-baby
Health A-Z for pregnancy, babies and toddlers.

Netmums
www.netmums.com
Advice, shared experiences and chat room for mums.

Osteopathic Centre for Children, London, UK
Tel: 0208 875 5290

www.occ.uk.com

Charity providing a checking service and the gentle manipulation sometimes needed to realign the bones of a baby's or young child's skull displaced during the pressures of birth.

The Parent Infant Partnership UK (PIPUK)
www.pipuk.org.uk

PIPUK is developing specialised parent/infant relationship teams across the UK. (Known as Rare Jewels!) They work closely with parents who are experiencing difficulties in their relationships with their babies from conception to age two. Their vision is to ensure that all babies experience a sensitive, nurturing relationship to lay the foundations for lifelong mental, physical and emotional health.

Association for Post Natal Illness (APNI)
Tel: 0207 386 0868

www.apni.org

Offers one-to-one live chat online, telephone and email support to mothers suffering from postnatal illness. The service is staffed by volunteers and there is no charge.

Unicef (UK) Baby Friendly Initiative
0207 375 6144/6052

www.babyfriendly.org.uk

Offers support and training to promote breastfeeding in organisations, such as hospitals, and offers lists of units in your area who run the Baby Friendly Initiative.

Womens Health
www.womenshealth.gov/pregnancy/you-get-pregnant/preconception-health

Fertility and pre-conceptual care.

WATCh? – What About the Children?
Tel: 0845 602 7145

www.whataboutthechildren.org.uk

Speaks out for the emotional needs of the under threes – for the love, time and security of being with Mum. WATCh? publishes leaflets and papers on the needs of babies and young children, based on research into the effect of separation stress on brain development and the nervous system.

Wildfare
Tel: 0117 382 5396

www.wildfare.co.uk

Nutrition for natural fertility.

24 Weeks Plus

www.24weeksplus.com

Helping premature babies and their families. They have a useful 'Links' page giving you a comprehensive range of organisations able to help with conditions that might affect your pregnancy or your baby's health.

HELPFUL BOOKS

Your Amazing Newborn by Phyllis and Marshall Klaus

Through over 120 stunning photographs, this book shows us how babies comfort themselves in the womb and their extraordinary abilities in the first two weeks of life. They vividly show a baby's first reaching, first gazing, first sparks of recognition and how they nestle into their parents' embrace as though they had practised for years. All these are the start of lifetime bonds.

Baby Bliss by Dr Harvey Karp

The first three months and beyond. Describes the Calming Reflex and the Cuddle Cure to help you calm your baby in a matter of seconds, relax and sleep through the night.

The Baby Book: Everything You Need to Know About Your Baby from Birth to Age Two by William and Martha Sears

Comprehensive guide to infant and childcare ranging from having a safe birth to the special needs of newborns, feeding and nutrition, common illnesses.

Baby Massage for Beginners – Johnson & Johnson – a printout available from the Baby Centre website:

www.babycentre.co.uk/baby/dailycare/massageforbeginnersprintable

Baby Massage: The Calming Power of Touch by Alan Heath and Nicki Bainbridge

Easy-to-learn massage techniques that soothe and promote wellbeing. Suitable for parents who want information about massaging their baby before they attend a course, or for those who cannot find classes running locally.

Baby Massage: Expert Know-How at Your Fingertips by Gayle Berry

Baby Massage: The Magic of the Loving Touch by Amelia D. Auckett

Baby Science: How Babies Really Work! by Ann Douglas

Baby Shock by Elizabeth Martyn and Relate

Ba

by Yoga: Gentle Exercise for Babies, Mums and Dads by Françoise Barbira Freedman
Exercises for mother and baby together. Especially for new mothers who need to exercise with care.

Beautiful Babies, Fabulous Families, Wonderful World by Belinda Barnes
Restoring natural fertility and creating happy, healthy babies.

Beginning Life: The Marvellous Journey from Conception to Birth
by Geraldine Lux Flanagan
A unique window into the womb through stunning photographs and sensitive descriptions.

Being Born by Sheila Kitzinger MBE
Documentary story of the nine-month journey from conception to birth. Outstanding photographs by Lennart Nilsson.

The Better Pregnancy Diet by Patrick Holford & Liz Lorente
Information to enable mother and baby to remain healthy throughout pregnancy and early motherhood.

Birth and Our Bodies: Exercises and Meditations for the Childbearing Year and Preparation for Active Birth by Paddy O'Brien

Birth & Relationships. How Your Birth Affects your Relationships
by Sondra Ray & Bob Mandel

Birthing from Within: An Extra-Ordinary Guide to Childbirth Preparation
by Pam England and Rob Horowitz
Exercises and activities such as meditation, painting and writing to help you discover yourself and face any particular fears you have during pregnancy. Also introduces the basic skills of baby handling and baby calming, once your baby is born.

Birth Without Violence by Frédérick Leboyer

The Blossom Method – The Revolutionary Way to Communicate with Your Baby from Birth by Vivien Sabel
Helping you understand your baby's body language and 'tongue talking' signals so you can recognise what your baby needs and learn how to communicate with him from birth.

Children Cheerfully by Kirsty Williams and Ingrid Brown
A very highly recommended small, ring-bound, wipeable book with outstandingly valuable and simple advice, routines and recipes to bring happiness and harmony to parents with their babies and toddlers – helping them gain confidence fast by avoiding many worries and insecurities.

The Continuum Concept (Arkana): In Search of Happiness Lost by Jean Liedloff
Instinctive nurturing and childraising through touch, trust and community. Practical ways to regain a natural wellbeing for ourselves and our children, as practised over thousands of years by our forebears.

Effective Birth Preparation: Your Practical Guide to a Better Birth by Maggie Howell (author of *Natal Hypnotherapy*)
A birth preparation book that focuses on feelings and emotions rather than on the technicalities of birth. A complete how-to-deal-with-fear toolkit for all pregnant women.

Empty Cradle, Broken Heart: Surviving the Death of your Baby
by Deborah L. Davis

Fathers-To-Be Handbook: A Road Map for the Transition to Fatherhood
by Patrick M Houser
www.fatherstobe.org
Real stories, solid research, ideas and encouragement for expectant and new dads. Innovative ways to give support to the mother of their child, be involved in the birth and grow together as a strong and loving family.

Fathers Feel Too by Andrew Don
A book for men by men on coping with the death of a baby.

The Good Birth Companion: A Practical Guide to Having the Best Labour and Birth by Nicole Croft
Wise advice and simple skills from an experienced doula to prepare you mentally and physically for the birth and ensure you have a positive experience, whether you have a natural birth or need medical intervention.

Ina May's Guide to Childbirth by Ina May Gaskin
This book by America's leading midwife is an intuitive guide to childbirth. It teaches what really happens during labour, how to create a safe and comfortable environment for birth, how to maximise your chance of an unmedicated labour and birth. It also describes the risks of anesthesia and caesareans – what your doctor does not necessarily tell you.

Infant Massage: A Handbook for Loving Parents by Vimala McClure
www.touchneeds.com
Vimala set up the International Association of Infant Massage and worked in one of Mother Teresa's baby hospitals in India.

Mothering the Mother: How a Doula Can Help You Have a Shorter, Easier and Healthier Birth by Marshall H. Klaus

Nurturing New Families: A Guide to Supporting Parents and Their Newborn Babies by Naomi Kemeny

Mothering the mother, listening to and supporting her in the first weeks after her baby is born while she recovers her strength and responds to her baby's needs. Warm mother-and-baby-postnatal care by a postnatal doula, a family member or friend.

The Oxytocin Factor: Tapping the Hormone of Calm, Love and Healing by Kerstin Uvnäs Moberg

Oxytocin is the powerful hormone involved in love, sex and childbirth, as well as feelings of relaxation and calm.

Postnatal Yoga by Françoise Freedman and Doriel Hall

Illustrated guide to yoga postures especially for mothers with new babies. Exercises are included to help mothers recover from caesarean, episiotomy, giving birth to twins, and special routines are given for both bottle and breastfeeding.

Praying for Your Unborn Child by Francis and Judith MacNutt

Why Babies Cry – What Every Parent Needs to Know, Kindle Edition, by Graham Kennedy

Explores the five reasons why babies cry. Helps parents who want to understand what their babies are trying to tell them and what they can do to calm them.

Yoga for Pregnancy by Françoise Barbira Freedman

DVDS

The Healing of Birth

Invitation to Intimacy DVD, 53 mins. Elmer Postle. Owl Productions – www.wholebeingfilms.com

A beautiful film looking at the awareness of infants in the moment of birth and the time around it.

More Than Words Can Say

www.brazelton.co.uk/resources

This DVD has been made by the Brazelton research team at Addenbrooke's Hospital in Cambridge – part of the Brazelton Network worldwide. It demonstrates to new parents their own baby's competence, understanding and wonderful response and recognition of their presence and their voices from the moment of birth. It helps parents to notice and therefore better understand their baby's behaviour and movements from the very beginning. They begin to pick up the cues of trust and loving expectation that is unfolding in their child during every moment the baby is awake and alert.

MUSIC TO HELP YOU AND YOUR BABY CALM DOWN AND SLEEP

Music for Dreaming and Music for Dreaming II
by Cherie Ross and The Melbourne Symphony Orchestra
Streaming, MP3 or Audio CD. Lullabies played by flute, strings and harp. The uninterrupted gentle flow of music, reflecting the sounds a baby hears in the womb, can comfort you and calm your baby before and after birth.

Mozart's Cradle Song by Mary Jackson
MP3 download. Gentle instrumental lullaby.
Sleepytime Lullabies by Nicola Kerr
   Streaming, MP3 or audio CD. A mix of traditional and modern cradle songs specifically designed to put babies and infants to sleep. Melodies, nature sounds and familiar lullabies, combined with heartbeats and the sonic vibrations of the womb.
   Some of the above can be obtained from Touch-Needs Ltd
   www.touchneeds.com

PRODUCTS

Bednest (highly recommended)
www.bednest.eu for new and refurbished Bednests and accessories.
Folds flat. Crib separates from base so can be moved to another room to be in constant reach. Levels to any height of bed. With tilting mechanism.

For other rcommended co-sleeping bedside cribs:

www.madeformums.com/reviews/8-of-the-best-co-sleeping-cots-and-cribs-for-safe-sleeping/

www.theradar.com/features/best-co-sleeper-cots

www.sling-spot.co.uk
The sister service to Sheffield Sling Surgery and library. Slings and carriers of all kinds.

ABOUT THE AUTHOR

Sarah Woodhouse read Social Sciences at Exeter University and has been closely involved in the care and development of babies, children and young people all her working life.

In her early years she worked as a volunteer with the NSPCC in their newly developed Therapeutic Playgroups for mothers with their 'at risk' children. She became acutely aware of the loneliness and helplessness of many mothers and their difficulties in giving steady love, care and security to their babies and young children, the resulting harm being passed on from one generation to the next.

Sarah also worked with children on probation and as a home tutor with secondary school pupils excluded from school for disturbed or violent behaviour. She says: 'I learned more from those stressed and angry teenagers than from any other experience at that time. They taught me conclusively that the fear, loneliness and hurt suffered by babies and in early childhood has a dangerously negative impact on the development of their brains and personalities. This is likely to stay with them for their whole lives unless they receive one-to-one support during their school days.'

Sarah was on the council of Amnesty International UK, with a special focus on children's rights. She also worked for the Citizens Advice Bureau and with immigrant families at the Thomas Coram Centre in London.

For some years she ran a Saturday club for children with physical and learning disabilities – teaching them to swim, row, ride, paint, cook and enjoy various sports.

Sarah is the Founder and has been the Chief Executive of the charity *Right from the Start* for thirty years. The charity has been involved in extensive research and planning over many years. It has published the first four in a series of richly illustrated books for parents, teachers and professionals working with young families.